Property of

Irene E. Prochnow
1850 N. Lexington

St. Paul, Minn 55113

489 - 9129

THE ROCKINGHAM POTTERY

BY TERENCE A. LOCKETT
DAVENPORT POTTERY &
PORCELAIN 1794-1887

THE
ROCKINGHAM
POTTERY

ARTHUR A. EAGLESTONE
AND
TERENCE A. LOCKETT

NEW REVISED EDITION

CHARLES E. TUTTLE COMPANY, INC
Rutland, Vermont & Tokyo, Japan

First published 1964
Reprinted with amendments 1967
New, revised edition 1973

© Arthur A. Eaglestone and Terence A. Lockett
1964, 1967, 1973

Published by the Charles E. Tuttle Company Inc.
of Rutland, Vermont & Tokyo, Japan
with editorial offices at
Suido 1-chome, 2-6, Bunkyo-ku, Tokyo
in cooperation with
David & Chalres (Holdings) Ltd
South Devon House, Newton Abbot, Devon
England

Library of Congress Catalog Card No. 73-86799
International Standard Book No. 0-8048-1121-0

Printed in Great Britain

ACKNOWLEDGEMENTS

Our chief thanks are due to Mr. L. G. Lovell, F.L.A., Rotherham Borough Chief Librarian, and Curator of the Clifton Park Museum, for sustained encouragement and assistance throughout the preparation of the book; to Mr. Wells of the Museum for his unvarying patience in displaying wares; to the late Mr. A. Lane, Keeper, Department of Ceramics, Victoria and Albert Museum; to Mr. G. F. Willmot, Curator of the Yorkshire Museum, York; to the Master of the Royal Household, Mr. N. W. Millbank, for information bearing on the Royal Service, and also the Comptroller, the Lord Chamberlain's Office. To Mr. and Mrs. G. R. P. Llewellyn of Abergavenny for permission to examine their collection; to Mr. W. Mason of Rotherham for similar permission; to Mr. M. E. Redfern of Dorking, for a survey of his collection and other assistance; to Mrs. C. R. Ingham of Swinton, and Mr. and Mrs. G. B. Creighton of Darfield, for valuable documentary evidence; to Mrs. Thompson of Rawmarsh for access to her collection; to many others for similar facilities; and to the staffs of Sheffield and Rotherham Reference Libraries, for very real assistance.

Especial thanks are due to Colonel Nutter, of the Wentworth Estate Office, for permission to quote from the Wentworth Papers deposited in the Sheffield Central Reference Library, and to Mr. J. Bebbington, F.L.A., for his good offices in the matter.

For help in supplying information by correspondence, we would thank particularly: Mr. F. G. Taylor, Archivist and Curator, Minton's Ltd.; Mr. H. R. Singleton, Director of the Sheffield City Museum; Mr. R. Fastnedge, Curator, the Lady Lever Art Gallery, Port Sunlight; Mr. G. A. Tait, Assistant Keeper, Dept. of British and Medieval Antiquities, British Museum; Mrs. B. Greenberg, Publicity Dept., W. T. Copeland & Sons Ltd.; Mr. G. J. V. Bemrose, formerly City of Stoke-on-Trent Museum and Art Gallery; Mr. J. A. Harrison of the Lady Mabel College, Wentworth; Mr. G. N. Dawnay of Cardiff, for information concerning marked figures; and Mrs. Edgar Andrew Collard of Montreal, Canada, for the notice from the *Montreal Gazette;* and Prof. T. S. Ashton, for permission to quote from *The Economic History of England: the Eighteenth Century.*

Finally we wish to thank the Rotherham Municipal Libraries and Museum Committee for their generous co-operation.

A.A.E.
T.A.L.

FOREWORD: 1973

One of the more striking phenomena in the world of ceramic collecting has been the greatly developed public interest in Rockingham wares during the past forty years. For a time overshadowed by the general fame of the 18th century factories, at length it was recognised that the Swinton factory under the Brameld regime represented one of the last of the classic potteries, issuing porcelain and earthenware of fine quality well into the reign of Queen Victoria. For a very long time wares not made at Swinton—often the most garish of pieces—were placed on the market as of Rockingham manufacture—tea and dinner services, vases, cottages and poodles by the thousand. Now after careful research the field has been narrowed, the grain divided from the chaff. But in certain quarters the prejudice dies hard, a reversionary description being, "in the Rockingham style", which in itself gives little clue to real origin. Thus, the main preoccupation of the authors of this book has been to bring clarity and veracity to a clouded field.

Since the publication of *The Rockingham Pottery* in 1964, much research has taken place. There was, for example, in 1967 expert excavation at the site, in which shards dating from various stages of the Pottery's life were exposed. Activity on the part of the authors of this book, their friends and students of the subject have confirmed the major theories advanced in the first edition, and additionally have brought to light new shapes and patterns hitherto unrecorded—some of which are illustrated in the following pages. The extra illustrations, and the additional chapter on pp 138-145 which contains a detailed note of recent research and publication serve to bring the survey up to date.

The history of the Pottery (as recorded here) remains constant, no important additional information having been discovered. This narrative still forms one of the most detailed and revealing of potter-patron relationships in the field of English ceramics, of considerable value to the socio-economic student as well as to the general reader.

The authors are much indebted to many friends and correspondents who have generously exchanged information and provided illustrations (which are acknowledged in the captions). Too numerous to name individually, to all we offer our thanks. Finally, we would wish to thank the Rotherham Borough Libraries and Museum committee for their sustained interest in the subject, and our new publishers who have been unfailingly helpful in the publication of this revised and updated edition.

A.A.E.
T.A.L.

CONTENTS

PART I: POTTER AND PATRON

ILLUSTRATIONS

The pieces illustrated in Plates I-VIII are from the Clifton Park Museum collection. The photographs were taken with great patience and care by Mr. A. H. Gittens of Wrigley's of Rotherham. The authors are grateful to him.

The photographs of marks are reproduced by courtesy of *The Connoisseur* and Mr. G. R. P. Llewellyn.

Plates IX-XVI are of pieces from various collections. They are reproduced here by the courtesy of their owners whose names are given in the captions. Most of the photographs for these additional plates have been taken, with his usual skill, by Mr. Geoff Taylor of Hazel Grove, Cheshire, to whom we offer our grateful thanks.

PART ONE

CHAPTER I

HILL TOP

The pottery stood on the brow of a hill; the gaunt flint-mill chimney and the kiln-rims lifting over the serried roofs of subsidiary buildings. Over three hundred persons of varying ages and skills were employed in the gilding rooms, the burnishing and painting rooms, the grinding rooms and the numerous assembly shops. No less than half a dozen showrooms displayed to prospective customers objects ranging from the plainest wares to exquisitely decorated porcelain.

The pottery area of one hundred acres was flanked by woods; the largest, Wath Wood, containing a small coal-pit from which in the past supplies had been drawn. Now, a new pit at Elsecar, a few miles away, supplied the fuel. Pausing at the entrance before the stone-built print and counting houses, you looked across a well-wooded countryside towards the great park and house of Wentworth, the principal seat of Earl Fitzwilliam, the Whig oligarch of these parts, landlord of the pottery site, and for some time an indulgent patron.

Down the hill opposite, to the north and east, lay Swinton, a quiet village from which the pottery drew its first name. A canal wharf had been constructed here; a mile and a half beyond, skirting Mexbro', the River Don wound to the Humber and the sea. These waterways brought a constant supply of fine clays from the south, from Kent and Cornwall; by the same means finished products were dispatched not only to various parts of Great Britain, but to the Continent, to the Baltic shores, and through Riga to Russia.

Four roads converged on the pottery. From local villages, and even from more distant Rotherham (the nearest town), workmen trudged uphill through an open countryside, the majority dwelling, no doubt, upon the order of work that day; what they would find upon the bench, what new types to be fashioned. But a few—and these the artists— would in season pause to gather wild flowers: scabious and dog-rose, moonpennies and dandelions. Such dew-fresh posies they would take forward, first to copy in the pattern book, and later to transpose on decorated plates, dishes, spill-vases and the like. These men were always glad for the Spring.

The pottery artists were conscientious workmen, and they had need to be, for Thomas Brameld and his brethren were exacting masters. All flawed wares were mercilessly smashed and tossed upon the discard

7

heap, involving loss; but although the Bramelds were often served with bills they found it difficult to meet, their standards seldom lowered. They were perfectionists. This, their most cherished virtue, played a part in the final collapse; but they enjoyed lengthy periods of success, though fits of depression must have alternated often with times of high exultation. Today, their work in scores of public and private collections, stands in silent witness to an unquestioned artistic integrity.

In course of time the Swinton name was transformed into that of *Rockingham;* and after Hanoverian patronage, into *Royal Rockingham.* It is one of the minor ironies of history that this 18th century Marquis, twice Prime Minister of his country, should be more popularly remembered by the objects which the Bramelds fashioned, than by any measure for which he was responsible during the course of his political career.

* * * *

At no place among the potteries of England was the artist-patron relationship so close as in the Fitzwilliam connection with Swinton. Wedgwood, it is true, had many noble customers on his books, but the Bramelds were over many years encouraged and sustained by the backing of a great house; the estate a reserve upon which they drew, not only for financial aid, but other advantages deriving from personal association. Thus, the following account is one not merely of artistic enterprise, but a prime example of the 18th century Regency aristocrat, urbane, cultured, who, at home on his broad acres, was mindful of the creative artist in the midst. The relationship was within its limits a perfectly honourable one; the Bramelds suffered none of the humiliation which befell others in business. The Earl required no more than that they should exercise to the full such talent as they possessed. He imposed no conditions of servitude, and they for their part, strove to justify that trust. If in the end they failed, it was due to flaws and forces sometimes beyond their control.

CHAPTER II

BUTLER'S FIELD—AND AFTER

Many things happened during the fifth and sixth decades of the 18th century, but industrially, nothing more remarkable than the crop of potteries springing up in various parts of the country. Increasing material comfort, a distinct improvement of taste and manners set the demand, and to meet this kilns were built to bake the wares which soon became the commonplace of kitchen, parlour and drawing room. Bow started in 1744, Derby about 1750, Worcester in 1751 and Chelsea about 1743, Longton Hall in 1750, Lowestoft in 1756, and Wedgwood in 1759. By the end of the century one or two of these had fallen by the wayside, but the remainder, with increasing reputation, carried on.

Swinton, which began about this time, existed for four or five generations without attracting much attention in the pottery world. It was worked on modest lines, until, in its latter days, like a plant long retarded, it burst into singular achievement, enough indeed to earn a place in ceramic annals. The whole forms a fascinating story; but first we must turn to origins.

*   *   *   *

In 1745 a certain Edward Butler, of whom practically nothing is known, discovered on land adjoining the South Yorkshire estate of Charles the first Marquis of Rockingham, ceramic elements—principally a common yellow clay used for the making of bricks, tiles, and coarse earthenware. Oral tradition, running well into the 20th century, recalled that one little area of the working place was known as "Pancheon Field", so named since clay was dug out on the spot for the making of a mixing bowl, long in use for bread-making by northern housewives. Oral tradition too, outlined a tract between the kilns and Wath Wood as "Butler's Park", a faintly ironical reference to his occupation of the common land. Common land it must have been, for there is certainly no reference in the Wentworth Rent Books of a Butler tenancy of the Rockingham estate, although a tile-yard is registered in the name of another man.[1] Neither at this, nor indeed at any later stage, is there evidence to show that the Marquis, whose new mansion of Wentworth Woodhouse was one of the wonders of the north country, in any way supported Butler's venture. The man, completely on his own, built his kiln, set up his sheds, and turned to making the ordinary class of goods then in use—principally what was known as "hard brownware". Occasionally, perhaps in terms of experiment, wares other than tiles, jugs and pancheons were made. Jewitt mentions a "posset pot"

The common lands were enclosed at the end of the century by Earl Fitzwilliam and others.

bearing the date 1759, and having attached the fragment of a label inscribed "Swinton Pottery", made by or for John Brameld, who about eighteen at the time, was employed there.[1] But more of this Brameld later. . .

By 1769, the works must have been firmly established, renting probably some additional ground from the Wentworth estate. Arthur Young, who made in that same year, a detailed study of the Marquis's property, refers to a pottery at Rotherham in which "white, cream-coloured and tortoise-shell earthenware" was produced. "It employs", he related, "about two or three and twenty men and forty boys; the men are paid 9s. a week for day work, but much is done by the piece, in which they all earn more, up to 15s. a week. Boys of nine or ten years old have 2s. and 2s. 6d. a week".[2] This in all probability describes the condition of the pottery after it had been taken over in 1763 by William Malpass, who up to this year, had been proprietor of a small pot works at Kilnhurst, a neighbouring village. But that is as much as we know of Malpass. He too remains an obscure figure.

There is evidence, however, that in 1776, Wentworth House itself was drawing upon the pottery for supplies. This year, when Malpass was in partnership with a man named Fenney, we find an account headed "To the Most Noble Marqse of Rockingham"[3] in which 6 pint purple bowls at 5d. each, and 6 half-pint bowls at 3d. were dispatched to the order of Mrs. Eustachie Dubert, "Clark of the Kitchin" (sic). A second account later in the same year is here detailed in order to convey some idea of contemporary prices—

			s.	d.
2 Tureens and dishes	...	...	10	0
1 Tureen and dish less	...	...	4	0
4 dozen table plates	...	...	12	0
2 dozen table soups	...	...	6	0
6 sauce boats	...	...	3	0
6 large dishes	...	...	7	6
12 less dishes	...	...	6	0
12 less dishes	...	...	4	0
6 purple sugar bowls	...	...	1	0
			£2 13	6

[1] The pot was in the possession of Dr. Brameld, John Brameld's grandson.
[2] *A Six Months Tour in the North of England, 1769*, A. Young, Vol. I.
[3] The Second Marquis, later Prime Minister; Wentworth Papers.

We notice from the foregoing that the pottery has extended the range of its wares, due to the discovery and exploitation of finer clays.[1] It serves also as an index of the intake necessary to meet the requirements of a great house; that of the normal staff, and of the numerous tenants who dined in the place on Rent Days. In December, the gardens received 18 dozen pots for the price of £1.16.0.

On May 12th, 1778, William Malpass alone (for Mr. Fenney seems to have dropped out) sends in a further account—[2]

		s.	d.
18 large black jugs	at 6d.	9	0
12 less black jugs	at 4d.	4	0
6 Tort-shell dishes	at 4d.	2	0
6 Flatt dishes	at 3d.	1	6
12 Qt. Mugs	at 4d.	4	0
12 Pt. Mugs	at 2d.	2	0
		£1 2	0

There may have been some reduction here for quantity; a tortoise-shell dish for fourpence, and a pint mug for twopence must have been relatively cheap.

In 1778, Thomas Bingley, of a family of well-to-do local farmers took over, though one suspects that personally he did no more than place money in the firm, leaving management to others. The works extended and modernised, began to produce a variety of additional wares. Seven years later, a more notable development took place, when the Leeds Pottery uniting its resources with those of Bingley, assumed controlling interest. Who were the "Leeds Gentlemen" (as they were so often to be termed), and what their credentials?

Compared with the Leeds Pottery, Swinton was small beer indeed. Under the trade name of "Hartley Greens and Co." they issued a catalogue of 44 plates engraved on copper in which they announced for sale, wares enamelled, painted or ornamented in gold in any pattern; also with coats of arms, cyphers, landscapes, etc.; plain, ornamented, perforated and basket work, including services, vases, candlesticks, flower-stands, ink-stands, and spoons, etc. Their products were being exported in large quantities to Germany, Holland, France, Spain, Russia, and (it has been asserted) America. Despite the war with France which broke out in 1793, the national export of glass and earthenware to Northern Europe rose at a surprisingly swift rate,

[1] Open cast excavation during recent years revealed thick seams of fine clay running towards the pottery site.
[2] Wentworth Papers.

from 822,513 pieces in 1790 to 2,846,566 pieces in 1800.[1] Thus it is not surprising that in 1794, Hartley Greens should issue a catalogue with lists in English, French and German—later Spanish was added. It was a go-ahead firm.

Several partners ran the Leeds business, but management lay chiefly in the hands of John Green, a man of somewhat brash and forceful character. In 1785 he cast his roving eyes on South Yorkshire, and what he saw was good. The region around Rotherham offered distinct possibilities. There was a well-placed waterway system—the River Don was navigable to the Humber and the port of Hull; coal was plentiful, and men were eager enough to leave their rural occupations for the higher wages of industry. A second pottery here, drawing upon the tried experience of the parent body, using indeed the same compounds, moulds and general designs, would do something to meet an expanding market. What better then, as senior partners, to take over Swinton?

Green approached Bingley, who must have welcomed the proposition, and as partners trading under the name of "Greens Bingley and Company", they arranged with the Fitzwilliam Estate Office, a twenty-one years' lease of the premises. Among other partners, linked by marriage with the Bingley family, was John Brameld, a local potter who had grown up with the works; and being a man of some education, soon became correspondent for the Swinton side.

Some idea of Green's character may be gathered from the forceful muscle-bound prose of a letter addressed to John Brameld about this time—

"I should be glad", he writes, "if you and Mr. Bingley will look over the particular deeds, and if there is anything that do not meet your ideas, please point it out. When you have done this you may send them in a small box, directed for me; they never was in my mind when at Swinton, or should have done the needful then.

I have writ Charles with some sponges and. . .informing him I expect 4 Cm kills (*kilns*?) per week exclusive of China, which I hope he will be able to manage without increasing the wages.

Hope your biscuit kill turns out well. You have room now if you will but make neat goods, and be observing to get money; but it requires a strict attention to keep every weelband (*sic*) in the nick".[2]

For their part, the "Leeds Gentlemen" were to prove skilful manipulators of the financial wheelband before they had finished!

In the same letter Green speaks of consignments of flint by a Mr. Breary to Selby and Tadcaster. The reference here is of course, to the

[1] *English Overseas Trade Statistics, 1697-1800*, Elizabeth Boody Schumpeter, O.U.P., 1960.
[2] Jewitt. The Ceramic Art of Great Britain (1878).

12

Leeds Company's Flint Mill at Thorpe Arch. Flints came as ballast from Sussex to be unloaded at Hull or Selby, and thence by barge to Tadcaster, from which town they were transported by road to the Flint Mill. For some time, the Swinton works must have secured ground flint from the Thorpe Arch Mill,[1] thus increasing its dependence on Leeds. Green also offered Brameld from himself and partners a commission of five per cent on "all wearing apparell sould (*sic*) in your works". This last reference referred, no doubt, to the sale of overalls to workmen and apprentices.

There is also evidence to show that the Wentworth Estate was willing as far as possible, to assist the new venture. They provided timber for the construction of new buildings. The area rented included a quarry from which stone was cut; and a small farm which provided stabling, grazing, and hay for the draught animals. In 1793, the Earl consented to the sinking of a coal-pit in the adjacent Wath Wood. Writing to Fitzwilliam in December of that year, Charles Bowns, the Agent, reports —"The Boring at Wath Wood goes on with great diligence, but with great difficulty...a soft bind along with water keeps clogging up the hole to such a degree that the men are scarecely able to move the rods ...I was there on Friday, and the depth was then ninety yards, which is two yards deeper than when coal was expected to be found; on Saturday they only got four inches, and I have not heard of (from) them since, but if they had pricked the coal I should have been let know".

At the end of January, Bowns stopped the boring for the time being, but he did intend to proceed. It would be necessary (he stated) to work for double shifts—days and nights—until coal was found.

Later, when rentals due from the pottery proprietors to the Earl may appear somewhat heavy, the use of farm, quarry and coal-pit ought to be remembered.

*   *   *   *

For the time being it would seem that Leeds and Swinton worked in harmony. John Green seems to have kept closely in touch with John Brameld, as a letter of April, 1788, from the former to the latter, indicates. Henry Ackroyd, one of the four principal partners in the Leeds Pottery had just died. "Our worthy friend Ackroyd", writes Green, "is dead, and I doubt not but is alive again. It was a pleasant reflection to me, being one of the pall-bearers to think I was bearing the cover over a dead Carkass (*sic*) whose soul I had not the least doubt was in heaven. He left this world with as great a Composer (*sic*) and Confidence in his future state as was possible for a man to do, and I sincerely wish that you and me may be as well prepared as friend Ad. (*Ackroyd*) for a future state".

[1] The mill is still standing, the old machinery comparatively intact.

These pleasantly pious reflections, however, in no way impaired John Green's business acumen. We are told that he became acting manager of the Swinton works, and an identity of production between the two potteries at once took place. Jewitt claimed the possession of some original drawings and designs on which the numbers for each of these works were given—for instance, in teapots, Leeds No. 149 was Swinton No. 68; Leeds 133 was Swinton 67; Leeds 252 was Swinton 71, and so on.

The connection with Wentworth House increased. During the months of May, June, July and August, 1793, the pottery supplied no fewer than 506 pieces, the range and price of these not without interest—

Bought of Greens Bingley & Co.

60 large garden pots	at	5d.
40 smaller garden pots	at	2d.
60 smaller garden pots	at	1½d.
96 smaller garden pots	at	1d.
96 smaller garden pots	at	½d.

12 large pudding pots	at	1/-
12 coarse garden pot stands	at	2d.
12 black chamber pots	at	2d.

12 hand basons	at	10d.
12 bottles	at	10d.
12 chamber pots	at	10d.
60 pudding pots ranging from 6d. to 1½d. each		

4 oval china bakers	at	3s. 6d.
4 larger china bakers	at	7s. 6d.
6 quart china bowls	at	3s. 6d. [1]

It goes without saying that wares were distributed throughout local towns and villages, but Wentworth must have provided the largest single order.

Owning this wide desmene, the second Earl Fitzwilliam had in 1782, inherited the estate from his uncle, the Marquis of Rockingham. A classic mausoleum housing a life-size statue of the dead statesman by Nollekens, attested some part of the nephew's veneration which seemed not to diminish with the passing years. A Fitzwilliam medallion issued by admirers in the early nineteenth century, bears on the reverse side —"Heir to the virtues as well as to the estates of his uncle, Charles, Marquis of Rockingham, and not more nearly allied to him by proximity of blood than by similarity of manners".

[1] Wentworth Papers.

PLATE I

a.   Green-glazed plate. Diam. 8¾in. (BRAMELD +5 *impressed*);
     Earthenware jug. Ht. 3½in. (ROCKINGHAM *impressed*); Green-
     glazed plate, leaf pattern. Diam. 7½in. (BRAMELD +4 *impressed*).
b.   Earthenware dish, green "Don Quixote" transfer, 12¼in. × 10in.
     (BRAMELD +1 *impressed*); Earthenware dish, blue "Woodman"
     pattern transfer. 12½in. × 9½in. (BRAMELD +1 *impressed*).

PLATE II

a. Cadogan pot. Ht. 6½in. (ROCKINGHAM *impressed*); Coffee/chocolate pot. Ht. 4½in. (ROCKINGHAM *impressed*); cane-coloured stoneware jug—relief decoration in blue. Ht. 6½in. (BRAMELD in cartouche, mark 26).

b. Earthenware dish, blue "Castle of Rochefort" pattern transfer. Diam. 9½in. (BRAMELD + *impressed*); Earthenware dish, blue "twisted tree" pattern transfer. Diam. 10½in. (BRAMELD *impressed* and printed mark 29).

This was no formal encomium. All who met and knew Fitzwilliam testified to his common humanity, his generosity, his genuine interest in the people of the region. He was approachable. Young James Montgomery, a stranger waiting by the roadside, presenting one of his own poems, was at once handed a guinea from his Lordship's washleather purse. The Earl could be seen frequently walking in the streets of Rotherham, calling at the bank or on tradesmen, chatting familiarly with citizens. He was, of course, immensely rich, but he never allowed— or seemed to allow—this wealth to impose an artificial barrier between himself and those less favoured.

In politics, Fitzwilliam had enjoyed one hour of dubious fame. Appointed by Pitt, Lord Lieutenant of Ireland late in 1794 he had assumed office to the background of the vexed "Catholic Question". In a hot-bed like Dublin, he was warned against the imprudence of introducing official legislation on the subject. Moved however by his genuinely liberal principles, he ran counter to instructions. Almost immediately after his arrival he dismissed the Commissioner for Revenue, and the Secretary at War; and after receiving addresses from both Catholics and Presbyterians promised full civil equality, introducing a bill to that effect on February 12th, 1795. The Earl had been in actual office only three weeks!

George the Third was angry, and the Government distinctly embarrassed. William Pitt, who could not defy his monarch, nor ignore the Anglo-Irish and a considerable body of home opinion, decided to recall Fitzwilliam. Sadly, the Earl's closest colleagues agreed. So back came one whom the Irish regarded as a deliverer, and Pitt a stupid bungler. The Earl, who never again attained the same political prominence, was perfectly sincere in his attempt to grant emancipation to the Catholics, but the time was not ripe. Like so many impulsive idealists, he imagined that he had only to take a stand, for all to rally round. The effect in Ireland was bad, since the Catholics felt they had been betrayed. As for Fitzwilliam, he returned to his estates in England, and never again assumed a major position in national affairs.

Almost a quarter of a century later, he was once again to invoke official displeasure. In 1819, after calling for a public inquiry into the "Peterloo" massacre, he was dismissed by the Prince Regent from his post as Lord Lieutenant of the county; dishonour (it may be added) he bore with equanimity and grace. He remained—in the eyes of his own people at least—an object of enhanced affection.

One incident, completely characteristic of the man, had wide circulation.

A farmer complained to Earl Fitzwilliam that the Hunt had almost ruined his Spring sowing. Asked to name an estimated amount of damage he (the farmer) indicated £50, and was immediately recompensed.

Later that year, the same farmer presented himself at Wentworth, and returning the £50 explained that his crops far from suffering as he had anticipated, had turned out extraordinarily good.

The Earl, listening to the story, rejoined, "Good—good—this is as I like it—man to man". He then inquired particulars of the farmer's family, and suddenly leaving the room returned with a warrant for £100, which he pressed in the farmer's hand. "When your son reaches the age of twenty-one", said the Earl, "give him this, and relate to him the circumstances in which it arose".

So much for the peer; now for the potter.

* * * *

As we have seen, John Brameld had been at Swinton many years. A working partner, in 1786, he brought his eldest son William, then aged fourteen, into the business, presumably as an apprentice. In 1801, Thomas, the second son, again at the age of fourteen, was taken in, but by this time business had so slumped that William applied for work in Staffordshire. He was unsuccessful, for (as John Brameld himself observed some years later in a letter to the Earl) "what manufacturer would take into his bosom a youth whose family was engaged in a similar trade to their own?"

There seems to have been more in the slump just mentioned, than meets the eye, for with this must be linked certain extramural activities of the Greens Bingley concern. In 1800 John Green had purchased a plot of waste and swampy land down the hill beside the canal. A small pottery had been worked there, but now considerable extensions were being made, and at the new "Don" works, articles were produced— perforated dishes, plates, spoons, flower-vases, cruets and stands, etc., in the same form as those of Leeds. What did this new activity portend? True, the lease of the hill-top pottery had still six years to run; but was the artful Green family laying up treasure in heaven, or in other words diverting trade to the new venture in anticipation of abandoning Swinton? And in what condition would the Swinton pottery be left? John Brameld, whose fortune was tied up with the familiar place, became increasingly apprehensive. Swinton was being slowly starved of orders— "allowed to run down", as he later put it, much of it "so long lain dead".

His first move was, by some means, to buy out the Leeds shares, and to this end he enlisted the services of Mr. Charles Bowns, the Earl's agent, as negotiator. But nothing came of the matter. The Leeds gentlemen were unwilling to sell. For them, the time was not ripe. So John Brameld had the mortification of seeing the manufactory, in which his all of capital and labour was placed, being slowly starved to death. What would the expiration of the lease bring?

The early days of the century were fraught with additional anxieties, for always in the background dragged the interminable French war. In

16

1803, among those volunteering men and vehicles for the use of the Government "if an invasion should take place on the appearance of an enemy upon ye coast", were Greens Bingley & Co. with the offer of "2 waggons 8 horses and 2 men with necessary implements—Wm. Scorah, Junr., to superintend and manage with an assistant".

Bramelds also served in the Militia—William, Captain, and Thomas, Lieutenant, in the Wath Wood company of the Rotherham Volunteer Infantry. Other potters were in the ranks, and once—only once—on the night of August 18th, 1805, they marched to Doncaster at the false alarm of an enemy landing. The Bramelds certainly responded to the call of duty, but their attachment to arms was only transitory.[1]

The pottery problem remained unsolved. . .

The full story of this affair is told by Asline Ward of Sheffield; see his *Diaries*.

CHAPTER III

THE LEEDS GENTLEMEN

That Lord Fitzwilliam was interested in the development of his estate goes without saying. He was to open new coal-pits, giving employment to hundreds of workmen; he backed local iron foundries, and later, the building of new railways. A study of the estate papers reveals an astonishing range of support for public works and charitable institutions. Fitzwilliam himself, owning estates both in England and Ireland, passed frequently from one to another. Actively engaged in Whig party politics, he could hardly be expected to employ himself with every detail of his tenants welfare; faithful bailiffs and agents were to do this for him—we have already noted Mr. Charles Bowns—but on every issue his was the deciding voice.

The Earl must have been acquainted with the Bramelds for many years. The pottery apart, two members of the family were commissioned officers in the militia; the constant flow of manufactured wares into every quarter of the great house would be sufficient reminder.

The lease of the pottery was due to expire in 1806, and the question which now presented itself was—with whom would the contract be renewed. One crumb of hope John Brameld held. In conversation with Mr. Bowns he had been assured that if a new lease were to be taken "it would not be in favour of the Leeds gentlemen."

So far, so good. But that did not solve the immediate problem of how the Leeds interest was to be purchased. Where was the money to come from? Apart from his present invested share, John Brameld had little or no capital to fall back upon, nor was he at the moment in touch with a responsible backer.

On the last day of 1805 the Leeds people showed their hand. Thomas Bingley, William Hartley and James Winter Butterworth representing the controlling interest, proposed that after a valuation of the property, payment must be made for the shares they held, such payment to cover a period of three years, and further, that "Messrs. John and William Brameld find sufficient security for the payment of the said moneys." In laying down these conditions the Leeds men must have known that the Bramelds had not the means to meet them.

As a last resort John Brameld decided to make a personal appeal to Earl Fitzwilliam. Next day he wrote setting out the full position, and making a comprehensive proposal of his own. Formal, but deeply emotional, the letter is worthy of reproduction in full—

Swinton, Jan. 1st, 1806.

My Lord,

It is not without a considerable degree of pain that I feel myself under the necessity of intruding upon Your Lordship's

18

attention a second time on the Swinton Pottery affairs—to a person of Your Lordship's eminent Rank and Dignity the private affairs of individuals must indeed be trifling, and nothing but the peculiar hardships of my situation together with a sense of Your Lordship's feeling compassion for your fellow creatures could have emboldened me to address you in this manner.

Upwards of fifty years of my life have been spent in anxious and persevering industry and in which I am now grown grey; every branch of my family (a wife and six children) have too as their years enabled them, contributed their share towards that fund of earnings and economy by which we hoped to raise ourselves to a decent degree of respectability and usefulness in the world, but alas! these exertions have been counterbalanced by placing our little property and our confidence in the power of men whose systems have prevented its acquiring those fair and considerable profits which commercial capital in general does acquire, nay, has ever confined and cramped it so that it has not kept pace with the accumulation of common interest. As a proof of this and a very simple and convincing proof it is both of my former and present statement. The capital advanced and the interest thereon being five per cent annually to the 1st of January, 1801 amounted to £827 a share. Soon after and in consequence of the ill-usage experienced from our partners we offered them (Mr. Bowns doing us the favour to negotiate) our shares at £600 each being less by £227 than they cost in this way, but yet they refused to purchase, neither at that time would they sell or comply with any more proposal for the establishment of a free partnership. It is probable they feared that under the management of a man unconnected with any other work of the sort, Swinton Pottery might establish a free trade and become a formidable rival to their favourite and more fortunate work at Leeds.

The proposals made by Mr. Bowns on our part in 1801 being uniformly rejected by our partners, we had no other alternative either to leave our property in that helpless situation and wait until the expiration of the term in 1806. My two sons, the elder of whom had been in the business since 1786, and the younger since 1795, were during the greater part of the time since 1801 out of employment. Repeated applications were made in Staffordshire for a situation but without effect. We would not attempt to conceal the truth and what manufacturer would take into his bosom a youth whose family was engaged to a similar trade to their own? And thus unfortunately did we find ourselves situated and have so remained, while at the same time to gratify their prejudices our partners had placed at the head of the concern a person (as agent) who was an entire stranger to the business.

19

But I shall tire Your Lordship with complaints and it is the less necessary to trouble you with particulars since our partners have not presumed so far on the goodness of their cause to lay it before you (nor yet before Mr. Bowns) although they mentioned to us that they knew we had the favour of an interview with you. They refused to buy our shares, but they have at length consented to dispose of theirs, which they are now pleased to say they think the best mode for all parties as they wish to terminate the partnership amicably. On Monday they attended a meeting and made to us in writing the proposals of which we trouble Your Lordship with a copy enclosed herein. They at the same time showed an extreme urgency for a immediate, or at least a very early answer. We replied that it was out of our power to purchase, so that it depended on our friends to enable us to answer. They however would insist on expecting an answer in a week or ten days, because they must deliver up the land and the colliery on the 2nd of February.

To purchase their shares and carry on the work will require not less than 12 or 15,000£, and had the concern been carried on for the last twenty years as it might have been we should have been able, or nearly so, to accomplish this; but as it is we have now no friends at all, nothing but the property which has so long lain dead in the Pottery, so that after all our hands are fast behind us. To endeavour to remedy this we have applied to some gentlemen of property and respectability (we would not apply to any other) to join us as partners and make the purchase, but they have all pleaded an inability to furnish the money or prior engagements in other undertakings, and they have consulted their friends but find the allegation so general that they give us very little hope of success in extending our applications. If we are not enabled to purchase, we fear no other alternative but the breaking up of the concern and selling off the stock, which I fear will be attended by the loss of one half the value of the property, besides the injury sustained by the dismissal and dispersion of the work people of all sorts who are now employed and the breaking off the connections of correspondencies now in existence, all of which might be continued by a purchase and continuation of the concern. For Your Lordship's information I ought to mention one deficiency in the premises at Swinton Pottery (viz) the want of a Flint Mill. It has hitherto been supplied with its ground flint and glazes from the Leeds Company's mill at Thorpe Arch, and probably for a season might be supplied from thence or from the Sprotbro Mill near Doncaster, but all supplies of this kind would be precarious, and such mills belong to other potteries, and of course their own wants must be supplied with the first and

20

best, besides the profit they will charge on their commodities, and these for a considerable part of the material requisite in a pottery. The great Mr. Wedgwood has at his works a steam mill, and I think no place more suitable for one than Swinton Pottery so near to coal. I do not know the cost, but probably might be £2,000 or upwards. It would make the works very complete and add to that great consumption of Your Lordship's coal which the pottery full worked would make. Indeed the whole consumption of a pottery is in British raw materials and many of them surround the work in the midst of Your Lordship's estate at Swinton. When I contemplate the situation of that work, the place where I and several of my family have toiled many long years—yet hitherto without avail—and when I consider the hopes which have hitherto supported our spirits are likely to vanish and their expected advantages to be wrested from us—with the loss of one half of that which our labours have hardly earned—I can scarcely support the idea. May some friend step in and avert the calamity! It is only support we want, it is only money; we do not want the skill nor industry, our experience has furnished us with one and our natural habits impel us to the other. We feel confident we could (after a reasonable time to establish a trade) make the concern repay the reasonable expectations of any friend who might join us—even in the face of the extraordinary war.

I can perceive one mode, and at present only one, by which to escape the loss and evils of breaking up the concern, but I could not have brought myself to mention it, were I not encouraged by the paternal interest your Lordship has seemed to take in my welfare—that is for your Lordship to purchase the eighteen shares which the other partners offer and which I think they would sell on very moderate terms rather than break up. These shares you might hold without appearing to do so as the whole might stand in the name of my family, but this might be ordered as most agreeable to you, for really, My Lord, I cannot see any impropriety in your Lordship's carrying on your own pottery in the midst of your estate and working up the raw materials which it produces into a manufactured article universally useful and which now makes a considerable figure in the commerce and adds to the riches of the country. I believe there are instances of noblemen concerned in carrying on works of various kinds on their estates—indeed the working of a colliery is in some respects allied to a pottery.

If this is not too disagreeable an undertaking to your Lordship, it would indeed be to me an act of the greatest kindness, as it would effectually remove the difficulties I labour under. If on the contrary your sentiments run contrary to my wishes I must entreat your Lordship's pardon for the liberty I have taken in suggesting it. There would be yet one more way in which your Lordship could assist us, and only you, as we could not give security to any other person, nor would it be prudent to engage in that way except under the protection of one whom we could safely put ourselves into the power of—but as I have already trespassed so much on your patience, I forbear any more, and must now conclude with hoping to be favoured with your answer as early as you can make it convenient to enable me to reply to my partner's proposals for which they are so urgent.

I hope that your Lordship's health continues to improve and that the country may continue to be benefited by your Lordship's living to enjoy many happy New Years is the sincere prayer of one who remains

> My Lord
>> Your Lordship's
>>> already obliged
>>>> and faithful hble servt.,
>>>>> John Brameld.

Will your Lordship have the goodness to address me "to be left at the Post Office, Doncaster".[1]

Several points of this important letter are worthy of note.

In the first place, it is evident that Brameld had already made a tentative personal approach to the Earl, being received with consideration, and had left probably with the remark that since the pottery problem was a large matter, much thought should be given to it.

Secondly, the overtone is one in which John Brameld feels the definite hostility of the Leeds partners to an active and prosperous Swinton Pottery. He is anxious (one notes) concerning supplies from the Leeds Company's flint mill, which could at any time be cut off.

Again, he clearly identifies his own fortunes and those of his family with the works. His suggestion that the Earl should become a sleeping partner bears this out.

Finally, there is the bold plea that the Earl would by no means lose status if he were to follow the example of other noblemen (the Duke of Bridgewater for example) in supporting industry. Really, John need not have been unduly anxious. He was pushing at an half open door. He is also careful to point out the unemployment and distress of the work-people in the event of the pottery closing. The Earl would be touched by this, a decisive factor.

Broadly speaking, John Brameld pleaded well, but one imagines the trepidation with which he awaited a reply.

[1] Wentworth Papers.

22

The Earl, who had travelled to Milton, another of his estates, answered without delay—

Peterborough, January 5, 1806.

Sir,

Lord Fitzwilliam is so peculiarly circumstanced this morning that he cannot get time to write, but being unwilling that your letter should remain another post unanswered he has instructed me to say that though he can see the hardship of your case to the fullest extent, and every point upon which it bears, still his Lordship has to regret his inability to meet your wishes, either in respect to purchasing the shares, or in advancing you a sufficient sum to enable you to become the sole proprietor of the concern.

However, as far as any preference can be given in point of tenantry to this Pottery at the expiration of the Term, I believe that I may say with great safety, that it would be decidedly in your favour, and that you have His Lordship's hearty good wishes that you may get through this business to your satisfaction, to which (tho a stranger) I beg leave to add my own sincere wishes also, and to assure you that I know his Lordship's money engagements, in consequence of purchases which I have engaged him in, as well as inclosures, are got to such an extent as to preclude all hope of his being able to assist you.

With esteem and respect, I am, Sir,
Your most obedient
humble servant,
Henry Cole
Agent to Earl Fitzwilliam.

If you see Mr. Bowns you may make my best respects to him, and if you think proper you may show him this letter.[1]

The communication breathed goodwill, but fine words butter no parsnips! John Brameld needed money, or assurances of funds, at once. The impasse remained. His Lordship, favourably inclined though he might be towards the Bramelds, was not to be hurried.

A fortnight passed, and a meeting of partners to consider dissolution was called. On January 22nd, William Hartley, principal partner in the Leeds Pottery, representing himself and others; Ebenezer Green, another Leeds partner "for himself and others"; George Hanson, Thomas Bingley, and John and William Brameld met, when a set of resolutions was adopted. From the bearing of these it was plain that so far as they were concerned, the "Leeds Gentlemen" intended the Swinton Pottery to expire. The terms were drastic—

[1] Wentworth Papers.

23

1. That no more coals be got at Wath Wood Colliery.
2. That on the first of February next the Engine, Gins, and everything that is valuable belonging to us be removed from the
   Colliery to the Pottery premises, and that the pits be railed
   round.
3. That no more stone be got from the quarry on Wath Wood.
4. That the Willows be immediately cut and brought to the Pottery.
5. That the manure on hand be sold.
6. That the Crop or Crops on the Farm be immediately valued.
7. That the coals on hand be disposed of in the best manner possible.
8. That as many men be immediately discharged from the Manu-
   factury as can be conveniently done; retaining for the present
   only as many as may be necessary to compleat the orders already
   taken, and to make a few things that may be needful to assort
   the stock on hand.
9. That a schedule of everything belonging to the Colliery and the
   Quarry be immediately taken.
10. That these resolutions be carried into execution by C. Prince.[1]

In a word, to close down without delay. One can imagine the anxious
faces of the two Bramelds, father and son, as these resolutions were
passed. Did they vote against? They were certainly not in agreement.
(The role of Thomas Bingley is ambiguous. He appears to have been
regarded by Mr. Bowns as a Swinton rather than a Leeds gentleman.
Perhaps, growing old he wished to pull out with what compensation he
could).

Thus, work at the Pottery continued, but only in the limited sense of
completing orders and stock sets which were incomplete. The ship
appeared to be sinking. Men left in order to secure employment elsewhere. One or two went to Mexborough. So far there is no record of
attempt at purchase by the Bramelds of the Leeds shares.

Meanwhile, January passed into February. March came. The lease
was due to expire on the first of May, and the Leeds people were becoming most awkward. They certainly did not intend to renew the
lease themselves. Requesting a longer period of notice, they complained
that they had been unjustly treated! Poor Mr. Bowns faced by this
accusation, found himself in a difficult position. March 16th, 1806, he
explained at length the troubled situation to the Earl—again, what
letters of length, what scratching of quills, what dusting of undried ink!

My Lord,
   Being informed that some of the Gentm. of the Leeds Pottery
   intend to wait upon yourself, and as they appear much dis-
   satisfied, and particularly with me, I hope your Lordship will

---

[1] Jewitt; Charles Prince seems to have been the Leeds man on the spot. It
must be remembered that John Green passed to the Don Pottery.

pardon me for troubling you with a full statement of what has passed between me and them relative to the Pottery business, and which I conceive will be necessary for your Lordship to be apprized of in order to judge of the propriety of the claim intended to be made. 11th of May, 1785, Hartley Green & Co. made the proposals sent herewith, and on the 11th September following terms were agreed upon with them, as by Mr. Tenton's memorandum which accompanies the proposals. The buildings were erected, and your Lordship found timber according to the contract, and additional ones have likewise been made, and wood also found by your Lordship, but I think it probable that some erections may have been made for which timber was not allowed, and that I may have refused it, not thinking it proper to give wood for every building they might erect for their own convenience.

During Mr. Tenton's life the lease was not drawn, but after his death I prepared one and delivered the draft of it to the lessees, but they never returned it to be engrossed, which I apprehended was owing to the differences which frequently took place between the co-partners.

In August last, in consequence of the twenty-one years expiring at Candlemas and May day 1806, and the conditions of the contract having been as fully performed by both parties as if the Lease had been actually executed, and also knowing that the term of the Co-partnership expired at the same time (as I had been employed to prepare the Articles but which was never executed) I conceived it necessary on the part of your Lordship to come to a new agreement, in order to which, and as the only legal preparatory measure, *I delivered a regular notice to quit* to the Swinton Pottery Compy. which consisted of fifteen persons, and told Messrs. Brameld in September, and also Mr. Bingley at the rent day in November following, that my reason for so doing, was on account of the expiration of the twenty-one years, and for the purpose of coming to a new agreement, which I fully expected the lessees would have applied for, but I heard nothing from them until the 29th Jany. when Mr. Prince, one of the Leeds Company's agents called upon me concerning the quantity of coal got on Swinton Common; and upon my mentioning that I understood the Company were preparing to quit and had no intention of continuing the Pottery, he told me "that the Leeds Gentlemen thought themselves extremely ill and disrespectfully treated, by my giving *them so rigid a notice to quit,* that I should have written a *civil letter* to them as '*Gentlemen*'; but they were determined to obey the notice and apply to your Lordship for a compensation towards the loss they would sustain by being *turned out*—that they conceived any application to take the premises again, would be fruitless on account of the partiality which your Lordship and I had shown to Messrs. Brameld, by whom they had been told that unless they, Messrs. Brameld, were reinstated to *the management of the Pottery*, the Leeds Gentlemen would not be treated with, therefore they thought it high to time give up, if your Lordship and I were to dictate to them *who* should manage *their concerns*". He also said that the Leeds Gentlemen after receiving *such a notice to quit* would never *submit to go cap in hand* to apply for the premises again.

In consequence of this unexpected great offence which I had innocently and unintentionally given to these Leeds Gentlemen by giving them *a formal notice* (which I am now convinced was absolutely necessary and that a civil letter to fifteen parties would have completely broke up the trade at Swinton Pottery) and as they professed to be preparing to quit under erroneous ideas and mistaken principles, I was determined that they should not have any *just grounds* to assert that they *would not* be treated with, therefore immediately wrote to the *Leeds Gentlemen* the Letter No. 1.

> (The bearing of this letter was that "the Pottery would not be let to a company of whom some of the partners were interested in different commitments in the same trade". The necessity on expiration of lease for new conditions.)

Not receiving any reply to that letter, I addressed another to the Swinton Pottery Compy. on the 18th Febry.—see No. 2.

> (Letter 2. Ten days were given for a reply.)

On the 26th Febry. Mr. Prince called upon me again in consequence of a letter which the Leeds Gentm had written to those at Swinton, of which he allowed me to take a copy—see 3.

> (Letter 3. As the Leeds Company are not thought to be eligible future tenants, they ask for a longer period of notice than six months and reserve the right to claim from Earl Fitzwilliam some remuneration as "we are discharged from the premises".)

And in reply to that letter I sent one to the Swinton Pottery Compy. See No. 4 on the 27th Febry., from which time my correspondence with them as a Company has ceased.

> (Letter No. 4 Bowns points out that they have not applied for a renewal on the terms laid down, and consequently may be regarded as abandoning the premises. . .)

Whereupon the Swinton Pottery Company passes a resolution in which they assert that they are "very much injured" by the manner in which they have been "treated and discharged from the premises" This was by a majority vote; a dissenting opinion by John and William Brameld.

A few days since Messrs. Brameld acquainted me that the Company were arranging a division of their stock, utensils, etc., part of which they, Messrs. Brameld, wished to purchase in case your Lordship would please to accept them for tenants in future to the Pottery, to which my reply was that I could not agree with *any part* of the present Company, until such time as the *other part* of them had declined to treat, or their Term was expired and the whole of the premises given up, but that upon a dissolution of the Co-partnership and a separation of the Company, they were to have the preference.

Yesterday Mr. Brameld acquainted me that in consequence of the promised preference I had given them, they were treating with the Leeds Gentlemen for the purchase of the stock, implements, etc., and hoped that they would be able to come to an amicable conclusion, notwithstanding which, and the letters I had written, the Leeds Gentm thought fit among their other orders and resolutions to make that No. 5 (see above) which has induced me to trouble your Lordship with this faithful statement of facts, in addition to which I beg leave to assure your Lordship, that I have never given the least reason for anyone to suppose that the Leeds Gentlm would not be treated with, if they chose, but I have very strong reason to believe it never was their intention to continue the Swinton Pottery, if it was the *notice* would *not* have *prevented their application;* but its having been given, they make it a pretext, in order to obtain a remuneration for the loss they may sustain in giving up; but if the notice *had not been given,* I am fully pursuaded that as a dissolution of the Co-partnership must have taken place on account of the expiration of it, the Leeds Gentlm would have held over the premises another year; to the ruin of the old Tenants and the pottery trade on your Lordship's estate. If in any one instance they think proper to reflect on my conduct, I rest assured your Lordship will allow me the opportunity of indicating it, and have the honour of being

      My Lord

         Your Lordship's most obedient and

Darley Hall,   faithful servant

16 March, 1806.   Charles Bowns.[1]

[1] Wentworth Papers.

The final sentences of Mr. Bown's letter represent the pith of this tortuous correspondence. Without an official notice, the Leeds Gentlemen would have held on another year to make probable ruin perfect.

May 1st, the date of the lease expiration found the Leeds Pottery Company still in possession of the Swinton premises. Bowns allowed nearly three weeks to pass before he communicated, this time with Lord Milton, Fitzwilliam's eldest son, who in the absence of his father would be dealing with estate matters—

May 19th, 1806. Darley Hall.

". . . . I am sorry to inform your Lordship that the Leeds Pottery Company refuse to deliver up the premises at Swinton. They have ceased working, and I don't learn that they have any other motive for witholding the possession than that of taking away the trade, and injuring the pottery as much as is in their power. I must of course deliver ejectment to the tenants in possession, to which I expect they will appear, which will bring the matter before a jury at the next Assizes where I trust a verdict will be obtained, as I am not aware of any defect either in the title or the Notice to Quit, but in that case a writ of possession cannot be obtained before the Michmas Term. I have some reason to think that as the pottery works are erected upon the *Waste*, the Compy are encouraged to try your Lordship's title to them, and that such advice originates at Newhill. This being the case I must trouble your Lordship to return the minutes of agreement and proposals of the Leeds Pottery Company on their entry into the premises, which I sent to Lord Fitzwilliam when I wrote to him on the subject. The Rents were as well paid as usual. We have fine growing weather, and a great prospect of a plentiful crop of hay. . . ."

I have the honour, etc.,
C. Bowns.[1]

The lack of means, the procrastination of their late partners, and a general fear that they would lose all business connections, moved the Bramelds to an alternative suggestion. There were wheels within wheels. A pottery at Mexborough, about two miles distant, established in 1800, had been taken over by a Peter Barker, who by good fortune happened to be the son of Joseph Barker, manager of the Swinton Pottery. What more appropriate than to engage these works for an interim period? Thus once again John Brameld took up his pen to write another letter to the Earl, though one notes in what follows he makes no reference to the proprietory relationship already mentioned—

(No prefix—probably a copy)

"The Company holding Swinton Pottery having repeatedly

[1] Wentworth Papers.

28

manifested their determination not to retake the premises, J. and W. Brameld have digested a plan for carrying on—with the approbation of the Right Honble Earl Fitzwilliam—that work themselves on a reduced scale so as only to supply the British trade, but yet so as to consume about 2,000 tons of his Lordship's coal annually. To effect this it will require from £4,000 to £5,000 more than their share of the present capital, and his Lordship's former beneficent intimation encourages them to look with confidence to the kind and protecting support in furnishing them with this sum, or such part of it as they may stand in need of, when his Lordship may have it in his power to put them in possession of the premises.

The majority of the Company have not only treated Mr. Bowns's various offers with equivocation and disrespect, but they have refused to deliver up the premises at the time required in his notice; and one great aim of theirs seems to be to ruin the Trade of Connexions of this place and to transfer them to Leeds Pottery, by holding it shut up in the manner now doing they will be able to effect it, even in the short space of six months, unless some plan be devised and put into execution to prevent them.

There are two plans that present themselves for this purpose: one is to supply the customers with goods purchased at other manufactories in Yorkshire and Staffordshire, the other and much better plan is to take a work for a short period of time on a rent— and just now a most favourable opportunity seems to present itself for that purpose. At Mexbro' near Swinton is a small work built and carried on by some gentlemen who are ignorant of the business and completely tired of it, therefore will be glad to let the work and fixtures at a rent even for a short period of two or three years, and to dispose of the loose stock of goods and materials on moderate terms. By taking this place the trade hitherto carried on at Swinton may be transferred thither and preserved until these premises are liberated, when it can be transferred back again and probably improved by the addition of the present Mexbro' trade.

The workmen employed at Mexbro' are chiefly what have been driven from Swinton by the late events, and several other valuable old servants have been lately dismissed and are in want of employment. These may be employed and kept together on this plan of being taken back to Swinton when that work is ready for them, which will be a great advantage to the work as well as to the men. In doing this there will be no injustice to the Mexbro' proprietors, because they have made an indirect offer of their work for this purpose. This work at Mexbro' would in the meantime be supplied with coals from Elsecar being upon the banks of the River Don.

The only obstacle is the want of funds, but it is humbly hoped that his Lordship's goodness will obviate this by advancing part of the sum already mentioned, of which £2,000 will be sufficient at present, and with this kind help from his Lordship, J. and W. Brameld will be enabled to counteract the nefarious designs of the Rulers of the Leeds Pottery, and in some measure to repair those injuries and avert those various evils which they have heaped, and are proceeding to heap, on Swinton Pottery".

(unsigned, but in J. Brameld's hand)

Swinton, May, 1806.[1]

There is in this letter nothing like the stress, the desperate compulsion, of Brameld's January communication. It may be that during the intervening months the potters had received orally from the Earl, or possibly through Mr. Bowns, certain financial assurances. After all, it was in the estate's interest that the pottery should flourish, and who better in control than the competent eagerly awaiting Bramelds?

The letter which follows was endorsed in pencil, "£2,000 for Brameld."

Charles Bowns to Earl Fitzwilliam.

My Lord,
... I saw Mr. W. Brameld previous to his journey to town, when he informed me of the plan they wished to adopt for carrying on the Trade and keeping their present customers at Swinton Pottery; which I think feasible. I then understood from him that they might ultimately require a loan of three or four thousand pounds, but thought that about £2,000 would enable them to take the Mexbro' works. I am not sufficiently acquainted with the finances of Messrs. Brameld to judge whether or not £2,000 will be enough to enable them to carry on the trade, but if they don't ask for a larger sum, I hope it will; and if they succeed in getting the Mexbro' works, I think they will have a fair prospect of keeping their present customers, and carrying on the trade to advantage at Swinton Pottery when possession of it is got, but should not be surprised if a further loan should be requisite at a further period, and if that should be the case I trust that the Trade will be an ample security for the sum that may be necessary to *borrow* to enable Messrs. Brameld to carry on to the *extent proposed* which is to the *Country Trade only*.

[1] Wentworth Papers.

30

PLATE III

a. Royal Dessert Service plate, pale blue ground and lavishly gilt. Diam. 9½in. (Unmarked).
b. Dessert plate, "primrose leaf" moulding on rim, flower painting attributed to E. Steel. Diam. 9½in. (Red griffin).

PLATE IV

a. Teawares; cup, earliest recorded porcelain piece. Ht. 2½in. (Mark 39); Cup and saucer, grey ground and gilt. (pattern 1131, puce griffin); Cup and saucer, mid-blue ground with gilt. (Pattern illegible, red griffin mark 41).
b. Dish signed "*T. Steel pinxit*". 16in. × 14in. (Red griffin).

I have great confidence in their managing the business with the utmost caution and prudence, and that they will not attempt to push it beyond their means, which was the misfortune of the Co-partners on their first entering into the Pottery trade.

I have the honour to be
My Lord
Your Lordship's most obedient
Darley Hall,   and faithful
2nd June, 1806.   Chas Bowns.[1]

But it does not appear to have been necessary for John Brameld to transfer himself to Mexbro'. The position of the Leeds Pottery had by now become quite untenable. Faced with the prospect of an action at law in which they could hardly have hoped to succeed, with ruffled dignity they withdrew, and closed one chapter of dubious eighteenth-century business enterprise. What the Leeds Gentlemen had gravely under-estimated was the grim tenacity of the two Bramelds—that of John in particular—and in the background the strong, pervasive influence of a great Whig landowner.

The exact date when the Earl advanced a loan to the Bramelds, or indeed any final arrangement concerning purchase of stock and implements, remains obscure; but by midsummer they were accepted as the new proprietors of the pottery, already engaged in repairing the damage to trade caused by the tenuous skullduggery of their late partners.

*　　*　　*　　*

The year following, when in the course of the General Election, Lord Milton ran successfully against the Hon. Henry Lascelles of the House of Harewood, John Brameld (listed in the poll book as *Merchant*) and six other Swinton potters, journeyed to York, five of them to register plumpers for Fitzwilliam's heir, though the sixth with some show of independence, gave one vote to Wilberforce, who was also standing. But, gratitude apart, it would have been strange for John Brameld to have done otherwise. The pottery lay in the heart of Whig country.

[1] Wentworth Papers.

CHAPTER IV

THE BRAMELDS ALONE

Meanwhile, the war continued. Guns rumbled, infantry plodded, and gaudy cavalry clattered along the high roads of Europe. The British fleet held the high seas; but on the mainland, Napoleon passed from one strength to another. He imposed his "Continental System" against British goods, though surprisingly our exports increased during that period. There was some talk of large quantities of English pottery destroyed by the French when they captured Rotterdam. On the whole, however, recalling Mr. Bowns's emphatic declaration, we may assume that the Bramelds concentrated on the home market.

Covering this period of independent action, for they were now their own masters, little by way of documentary evidence is available, though it is evident that they manufactured to a close margin. A letter written by Thomas Brameld (presumably to William) throws a little light on working conditions at the pottery together with their financial situation. From "Hill Top" on Sunday afternoon, April 23rd, 1809, he states: "We have not *much* stock of printed, but could you procure more orders we could (by exertion) get more ware printed as now I cease to urge them for more work than their regular manner of working produces. We can also do more in enamel, Egyptian Black, Orange, Cottage, dips, and can without any increase in hands as to painters; we can also do more in it if we can only get ware made to paint upon".

Then follows a reference to the painting staff. "Elizabeth Barraclough went off last Sunday"—it would appear to London. "However, you need not hesitate to take orders for her work, as James Bullough, Abraham Nicholson and Shaw, the painters, all say they can do it, and wish to have it... However, my present intention is to have Anne Hodgson brought to do it (Dinah's sister). I shall first hire both of them until next Martinmas but one—my intention is this: first to receive Dinah (who is an excellent painter) and next to (*sic*) as an encouragement to Anne (who is a very good girl)."

From this it would appear that of the girls who were employed as painters, the work of one, Elizabeth Barraclough, was widely known and appreciated. The confused sentence of the last paragraph implies that Anne and Dinah were expected to work together, and after the fashion of the time, one to assist in teaching the other. The Bramelds certainly took on girl apprentices for painting. A bill to Mr. Brameld in 1812 indicates, "for clothing his apprentice, Mary Sailes, ½ Knaresbro' (*linen?*) 7/10½; 4 wild bore, 3/8; 7 striped for bedgowns, 7/-; caddus (*tape?*), thread, 1/-"

After referring to the difficulty of settling accounts with customers,

Thomas continues: "Last week's ready money was only £24, but it is no wonder when we consider how wet, cold and winterly it has been altogether. However, I find I have about £470 in hand and in the bank without calling upon them for above the usual £200, but as some of the debts have to run some time, I intend availing myself of their *liberality* as far as I think necessary".[1]

From this it would seem that the firm was working with modest financial resources, that outstanding debts were a problem, that girls had a definite place in factory practice.

For some time they laboured under real difficulty. The cost of ground flint must have been heavy. They no longer received supplies from the Leeds Company's mill, and were drawing from that at Sprotbro', and it may be, from further afield. Apparently the Leeds people had run into trouble, for as the following letter shows, certain of their workpeople had sought employment at Swinton. This raised the question of housing accommodation. There were too few cottages available. On August 25th, 1810, William Brameld, writing from the pottery to Charles Bowns, announces that they cannot at present meet the level of rent fixed by Earl Fitzwilliam, and from that subject passes to other pressing matters—

"The scale upon which we resumed these works was at first a very small one, so small that the assessments and other unavoidable payments upon the concern felt burdensome because many of them remained the same as when it had carried on to a larger extent—this induced us to strive at some extension, which we had effected by slow degrees, and then the stoppage of the Leeds Pottery afforded us an opportunity of drawing back some of those customers of whom that concern had previously robbed us. The application for employment of several of their disbanded workmen also afforded another facility as well as temptation to us of doing this to the extent of our limited capital would bear us out in. We are just able to carry on, but without a guinea to spare, and as our calculations and engagements are made prospectively and must influence our finances a year forward, we shall be unable to pay the advanced rent until the expiration of that time. We therefore hope that you will kindly state this to their Lordships, and that their goodness will induce them to defer the commencement of it until twelve months longer; by that time we shall be able to make such arrangements as, with the produce of our exertions will enable us to meet it and make our payment good.

We some time since troubled you with a letter on the subject of a Mill and dwelling houses—your answer was very obliging,

[1] Wentworth Papers.

33

but we have not proceeded farther in our application for two reasons, one of which was that you have been so much engaged of late—and another was that we have not been able to satisfy ourselves of the best construction of a Mill, and as we are cautious not to take any steps improperly we would rather defer it until we have opportunities of examining some of the existing Mills and their powers. We some time since drew drafts of a plan for a dwelling house, but we are not able to make an exact estimate of the cost, which however we suppose would amount to £800.

There is another description of buildings which we (or rather our workmen) are distressed for, and that is cottage houses; most of the houses in Swinton have been taken by other potteries and works in the neighbourhood as they become vacant (and particularly during the lapse of time when this manufactory was standing, and its workmen dispersed all over the country). We have in our employ several of the disbanded workpeople from Leeds Pottery most of whose families are obliged to remain in Leeds because they cannot run habitations in this neighbourhood. This is an increased expense to the poor men, and very uncomfortable for them as well as for their families nearly thirty miles off, added to which we are apprehensive that whenever Leeds Pottery so far resumes its activity as to offer them employment they will return thither and we shall lose the labour and expense we have bestowed in making them better workmen as well as steadier men.

On this subject as well as on the former ones we are quite unable to help ourselves—there are no cottages to be rented, and we have no money to build with. We have therefore no other resource than again troubling his Lordship and requesting that he will kindly add this favour to the others and build us a few cottages; two or three of them in particular would be doubly useful as Lodges at the different entrances to the Pottery, from the want of which we suffer considerable depredations upon our materials, the windows, etc.

We are willing to pay our noble Landlord the same proportion of rent for these cottages are we proposed for our own dwelling house. The number of families who are in want of houses are about nine—besides Mr. Robinson, our clerk.

I remain, with respect, etc.,
(signed) W. Brameld.[1]

It may be that the Bramelds saw in the misfortunes of the Leeds pottery something of poetic justice, but the situation (as we have seen) brought its own difficulties.

Wentworth Papers.

Nine months passed without any response from the Earl, but during that time Thomas Brameld had been inspecting steam-driven flint mills in the Potteries, and maybe elsewhere.

On May 21st, 1811, William Brameld, being in London addressed a letter to Fitzwilliam, who at that time was residing at his town house in Grosvenor Square. William explains that as his brother is in town also —was this purely co-incidence?—the two would like to make a personal call upon the Earl to explain more precisely than hitherto their pressing needs. This letter, prefixed simply "London" must have been written from an inn—

My Lord,
Although it has been the lot of my Father and his family to be troublesome to your Lordship at different times during a series of years, yet the humane attention you have always condescended to show us at the same time that it has impressed us with sentiments of lasting gratitude also encourages us to hope that your goodness will on this occasion likewise lend a kind ear to our requests.

These may be divided into four heads—an enlargment of the time before the commencement of the new rental upon the Pottery—the erection of a Mill to grind flint, etc.—of a family dwelling house on the premises—and of some cottages for our workmen.

We understand that Mr. Bowns had the goodness to mention these erections to your Lordship and that you kindly replied that if plans and estimates were made you would take them into further consideration. The last letter we wrote to Mr. Bowns was during the time your Lordship was in Yorkshire, and then we hoped he would have the opportunity of laying it before you left the neighbourhood, but it happened that he was a long time engaged in Town (although unknown to us). I therefore enclose a copy of that letter, and by your Lordship's kind perusal of it which contains our view of these matters at the period it was wrote, but since that time the difficulty of obtaining ground-flint, etc. has increased so much as to make it absolutely necessary to lose no further time in procuring a Mill.

We have corresponded with some persons, and as the matter became every day more urgent, my Brother (since I left home having been some time making our regular journey on business which in course brings me to London) has been twice into Staffordshire on this errand and has examined several of the best and last erected Mills by which he flatters himself he has become possessed of every satisfactory point of information to enable him to direct the erection of a steam Mill on the best construction

35

and calculated to grind every article requisite for the consumption of the pottery at Swinton. It was thought that it would be more respectful and satisfactory to your Lordship to wait personally upon you.

My brother has therefore met me in Town for this purpose, and we humbly request that (if it not trespassing too much upon your Lordship's valuable time) you would have the goodness to favour us with an interview when we shall be happy to give you every further information in our power as to the Plans and Expenses of the Erections which we wish to have made of which we are so needful for the welfare of your Lordship's Pottery.

With due deference and respect,
I remain for father and self,
My Lord, your Lordship's obliged
and very humble servant,
W. Brameld.[1]

It is reasonable to suppose that during this time the minds of Earl Fitzwilliam and his son, would be much more engaged with the political situation than by the affairs of the Swinton Pottery. The death of Princess Amelia, George the Third's youngest daughter, in the autumn of 1810, had upset the poor King's intellect for the last time, so that the chief business before Parliament in 1811 was a Bill to constitute the Prince of Wales, Regent.

There was accordingly, a great stir among the Whigs, of whom the Earl and Lord Milton were prominent figures.

They counted upon the Prince's former adherence to their own principles, and waited optimistically ("casting parts for themselves in the new administration" as Mr. Creevey put it) for the present Government to be dismissed in order that they might attain power. They thought (again quoting Creevey) that "the game was all their own again". And there is not the slightest doubt that one or the other, or indeed both, the Fitzwilliams were marked for preferment. So the Whigs waited... and waited... dwelling upon what for them was to remain a mirage. The Prince held to the old Ministers.

This was the situation when the two Brameld brothers, William and Thomas, rang the bell at Grosvenor Square. One feels the interview would not have been lengthy, but they must have secured satisfactory assurances, for in a comparatively short time a Flint Mill, a dwelling house for their own use, and cottages for the workmen, were erected...

* * * *

In 1813, William, the eldest son of John Brameld, died. For some years he had been his father's right hand; now, at his passing three other

[1] Wentworth Papers.

brothers occupy the foreground. (John Brameld, who must have been in an ailing condition, lived on until 1819).

The sons in question were Thomas, George Frederic, and John Wager. In numerous articles about the Pottery, writers, one copying another, have stated that in 1813 the three brothers "took over" the works; but when one reflects that George Frederic was only twenty-one in this year, and John Wager sixteen, it would appear that for a time at least, Thomas, who was twenty-six, carried the burden of responsibility. Nurtured in industry from childhood, men matured early in those days, but some considerable time must have elapsed ere John Wager with his samples and patterns, took the road as the firm's traveller, or indeed for George Frederic to be dispatched abroad as agent.

Thomas, who in effect directed the firm, dealt with all aspects of the business. Jewitt refers to him as "a man of exquisite taste", and all who came into contact with him made much the same observation. He certainly impressed the hard-headed Mr. Bowns. At times, the Earl too, must have fallen under his spell.

He lived hard by the pottery in the house they had requested the Earl to build for them, usually referred to as "The Cottage". A sizeable dwelling with a thatched roof, it stood opposite Warren Vale Road, and was so substantially built that it lasted well into the twentieth century before it was pulled down to make room for a more modern house. The windows had small diamond-shaped panes, and there were three doors on which were carved woodland scenes. A later occupant of the house remembered these carvings described as the work of an Italian painter once employed by the Bramelds; but since there is no record of a foreign craftsman at the pottery, the carvings may well have been the work of William Cowen, who under the patronage of Fitzwilliam, spent some time painting in Italy. The decoration may well have been done when he was laid off from painting wares.

The house included a wine cellar, which when Thomas Brameld left the place, was found to be full of bottles containing mysterious liquids having no connection at all with refreshment, and which were subsequently poured down the drain. These may have been elements for particular use at the pottery, retained by Brameld after the crash of 1842, conserved perhaps in the hope of some day resuming business. Perhaps the most intriguing spot in the garden was a stone cave known to later tenants as the "Fox Hole", a haunt, one gathered, which had been used as a strong room housing valuable wares. More than once in letters to the Estate Office, Thomas Brameld complained that from time to time they had suffered from the depredations of thieves, and considering the isolated site which the pottery occupied, and its close proximity to woodlands, this is not surprising. When in 1819 a village "watch and ward" was instituted, and Thomas Brameld became the leader, the pottery was made one area for supervision.

In his own district he was regarded as something of an eccentric. The story is told, that, believing deeply rooted fruit trees incapable of a full healthy yield, he caused all to be dug up, flat stones laid, the soil and the trees replaced, though what the outcome was we have no means of knowing.

But his heart was in the pottery. Like many another manufacturer of the period he lived beside his work; would consider no dwelling which did not afford easy access to the plant by day or night. When darkness fell and the shadows lay still among the kilns and storehouses, and the woods around were hushed, he would linger in the familiar place, his fertile mind evoking new vistas of activity, new shapes to fashion, new combinations of colour. Enticing avenues opened. Uncertain as he might be in money matters, he had the greatest confidence in his own artistic skill. One day perhaps, he would see his work in the furniture of kings. . .

* * * *

John Wager[1] Brameld (his second Christian name deriving from an old friend of the family who managed the farm), seems to have been, physically at any rate, the most active of the three brethren. Not only was he responsible for a good deal of painting—later he designed and worked upon the Royal Service and executed the Don Quixote panels on the first rhinoceros vase—but as the firm's traveller covered lengthy distances by road. For a period, he travelled through East Anglia, and made seasonal journeys to numerous towns in Scotland. One has only to envisage the primitive roads and inns then existing, to appreciate that canvassing for orders was no comfortable occupation. He must have been a man of personable appearance and manners. It was he who interviewed on behalf of the firm, the Duchess of Cumberland, the Duke of Sussex, and certain members of the nobility from whom orders were received.

Of all the family he was the least bound to Yorkshire. When the Rockingham Pottery discontinued, he decided to establish himself in London, at Bayswater, and exhibited wares in the Great Exhibition of 1851.

There is little information concerning George Frederic. At one time he was corresponding clerk of the firm. He was certainly sent for a time to St. Petersburg as agent. There is no record of artistic ability on his part, no designs were formulated by him, and apparently no wares decorated. He is overshadowed by his two brothers. . .

* * * *

The first decade of the century drew to a close. In 1812, Napoleon invaded Russia, and Wellington steadily beat the French out of Spain.

[1] Often misspelled *Wagner* by commentators. For details of his activities in London, see *The Connoisseur*, June, 1967.

Then followed the Dresden-Leipzig campaign, the Emperor's abdication, Elba, and Waterloo.

The Bramelds must have hailed the peace with high expectation, for in 1815 they built their largest kiln, named appropriately "Waterloo".

To the outward eye, during the next ten years, the pottery must have shown every sign of prosperity. The kilns and the flint mill smoked, and under the tall chimney of the latter building, the warehouses and showrooms, moulding shops, painting, burnishing, grinding and prism rooms, worked to full capacity. About three hundred persons were employed, though not all were artists and claymen. The population of Swinton, 653 in 1800, rose by 1820 to more than a thousand, an increase due mainly to the pottery.

Social habits and customs played their part. About this time tea-drinking greatly increased in popularity. In vain William Cobbett thundered against the wholly noxious, time-wasting, stomach-destroying beverage which people were pouring down their throats. Against tea he upheld the virtues of home-brewed beer as cheaper and more nutritious. But he was fighting a lost battle. In cottage homes as well as in middle-class parlours, cups and saucers were in great demand. In addition, farmers' wives and daughters looked for decorated cake-dishes, ornamental vases, dressing table trinkets and the like.

Impelled partly by a certain depression in the home markets, and despite the undertaking made in May, 1806 that they would manufacture for Great Britain only, after 1815 the Bramelds decided to turn to the Continent where for a long period English pottery had become famous for cheapness and reliability. During the eighteenth century travellers had asserted that every inn from Paris to St. Petersburg fed its guests on English earthenware. Now that the dogs of war were leashed, merchants might breath again, explore, expand. All roads seemed open.

The Leeds Pottery with which their father had been so closely associated, ran a continental trade via Hull and Rotterdam, but it was towards Russia that the Bramelds turned as offering the best market. That country was, of course, much in the news; the Emperor Alexander visiting London, had been the object of great popular acclaim—statuettes and busts appeared in great numbers—and there was a vast goodwill towards his country. There were certainly deep purses in Russia. The trend towards Westernisation would be favourable to an enterprising manufacturer.

Russia too had little by way of first class pottery. A factory started in St. Petersburg in 1744, and drawing upon Meissen skills, began eight years later producing porcelain figurines which began to rival the great Dresden centre itself. Tea and coffee sets in quiet domestic patterns were among the products of the first years; decoration at the outset simple, became more varied, but while St. Petersburg pottery deserved its reputation, the output was by no means large enough to meet the demand.

So George Frederic Brameld was sent with specimens to the banks of the Neva, and beyond a statement that he lived in St. Petersburg for some time, a baffling silence falls. As corresponding clerk to the firm at a relatively low salary, the move meant promotion. But in what special sense was he equipped? Was he master of the language? Was business carried on through English factors?

It is likely enough that the Bramelds' contact with Leeds proved of assistance. After 1800, when the Leeds foreign trade was principally with Russia, a man of that nationality named Ruperti became a partner. The Leeds agent in Russia at one time was a Mr. Barwick, and afterwards his nephew, Mr. Jubb. We have seen how in 1810-11 Leeds workmen drifted to Swinton during the eclipse of the former factory. Were the Bramelds able to draw upon some with an intimate knowledge of foreign trade, and thus make contacts for George Frederic? It is a reasonable assumption.

But so much for conjecture. That he secured large orders there can be little doubt; but how in a real sense was he able to gauge the financial credit of his customers? It may be that some Russian noblemen were as loth to settle accounts as their English counterparts. How far did George Frederic peer behind the facade of lackeys, uniforms, gold lace and fur? Doubtful as this may be, nothing is more certain than that "Brameld" impressed tea cups and saucers were set around steaming samovars, and that through Hull, boxes, or probably hogsheads, of carefully packed pottery, continued to reach the Baltic and beyond.[1]

John Wager Brameld had become the "home market" traveller. We shall find references to periodical "Scottish Journeys". He must have had numerous points of contact, including that with Robert Allen of Lowestoft who decorated unfinished Brameld wares.

It must not be assumed that these were the highly finished porcelain wares, which belong to the 1826-42 period. The Castleford and Ferrybridge Potteries also had a large trade with the Baltic countries and Russia. The Ferrybridge concern sold to Russia the finer and most expensive kinds of earthenware, cream-coloured, Egyptian black, and other kinds of fancy bodies, printed, enamelled and gilt. Napoleon's Berlin Decrees had ruined their trade.

CHAPTER V

BANKRUPTCY

The Bramelds had found the sunshine day, but as time passed, clouds lowered, and a storm from which they were lucky to emerge at all, overtook them. Trade expansion and exchange elements played a major part. The inner workings of the 1826 crisis have not been exposed before except in terms of general speculation, and conclusions founded upon too frail a basis. Jewitt states that failure was due to the cost of experiment in porcelain, said to have been started in 1820, to bone-china production, and to the transport of finer quality Cornish clays, etc., especially oxides for decoration. But while these may have been minor contributory factors, the explanation does not meet the case. The war too, has been cited as a cause of difficulty, but by 1826 its effects had long since passed. A further suggestion that the cumulative cost of artists they appear to have enticed from other firms embarrassed them. The real reason, however, was—as the Earl's agent who made a thorough examination of the books made clear—foreign losses to the extent of £22,000. We can only conclude that this applies to their large Russian commitments. For years Russian currency had been in a deplorable condition. During the war, when gold and silver were almost entirely withdrawn abroad, there had been a vast issue of paper money which had declined three fourths in value. In short, George Frederic Brameld returned from Russia with an albatross of debt around his neck. It was Wedgwood who announced, "I do not send my goods abroad on risque, but my foreign correspondents name me a house in England to accept my draft on my sending that house bills of lading of the goods being shipped, and that house being my guarantee, when the order is given, it is executed without loss of time". In addition while Wedgwood paid for carriage in England, he refused to meet the expense of shipping.

If the Bramelds had followed this sage counsel, they would have found themselves in little or no difficulty at all; but as pressure of debt fell upon them, they resorted not only to the expedient of borrowing at high interest rates, but also to the pernicious system of credit notes to tradesmen and others. Professor Ashton in his *Economic History of England: the Eighteenth Century* makes the position clear. "The dearth of money of all kinds", he observes, "had important social effects. In a century of economic expansion, manufacturers tended to lock up a high proportion of their resources in buildings, machinery and stocks of materials, and hold only a small proportion in ready cash. This proclivity had serious results in times of crisis, for it meant that when bills of exchange were no longer accepted for the payments of debts, the manufacturers and merchants had small reserves of hard cash upon which to draw ... A feature of circulation in the North West was

41

the large volume of small bills and promissary notes created by manufacturers for the payment of labour. Some were for amounts as low as eighteen pence or a shilling . . . the wage earners who received them passed them to local retailers who, when they had accumulated a sufficient amount returned them to the manufacturers in exchange for larger bills drawn on London . . . There was a strong temptation to exercise the power even when supplies of legal money were available".

From the large local debts which the Bramelds accrued, there is no doubt at all that they resorted to the foregoing means. Nor did contemporary banking and financial practice assist them. By 1819 deflation had caused a serious slump; by 1823 there had been some recovery. But in 1824 and 1825 a great speculative mania spread throughout the country. Foreign loans boomed, new companies were launched; following the repeal of the law against joint-stock enterprise, countless new banks sprang up, and new and old banks alike indulged in reckless advances and wholesale creation of public money. At last the bubble burst. The banking house of Pole and Co. stopped payment in 1825. A general run on banks began. Failure followed failure. One merchant house after another went bankrupt. And since the Bramelds were closely involved, the Swinton Pottery failed.

During 1825, and probably for some time previous, they were increasingly dunned by creditors. Oral tradition in the district recalls the shifts and stratagems to which they resorted in those desperate days. Two stretches of woodland already mentioned, flanked the pottery— one a coppice on the road to Rawmarsh, the other, Wath Wood, stretching beyond the main gates. In the latter were the disused workings of the coal-pit which had once served the concern. Now it was to prove of further service. When bailiffs were expected, the Bramelds in the dead of night removed their most valuable stock to this mine, while some part went into the coppice at the other side of the road. It is quite likely that the cave in the garden of "The Cottage" was used for the same purpose, but manufacturing in those conditions could not long continue.

In their extremity the Bramelds dwelt increasingly upon the possibility of aid from Earl Fitzwilliam. They remembered how he had rescued their father from an intolerable situation in 1806; how indulgent he had been in the meantime. They had a new venture in hand, that of the manufacture of porcelain, and they were confident that given capital to rehabilitate themselves they could turn out wares second to none in the country. But such capital would need to be substantial.

Meanwhile, bankruptcy proceedings went forward . . .

There is no record of any meeting between the Bramelds and the Earl, but one must have taken place—a "man to man" encounter much favoured by Fitzwilliam. The Earl (we may take it) was not unsympathetic. He asked the solicitor, Mr. William Newman to make a full report on the Bramelds' financial position. The completed text revealed a melancholy, almost hopeless prospect.

To Earl Fitzwilliam.

"Upon the examination of the books and accounts the annual statement appears to us nearly correct as we have been able to ascertain—

In tracing the causes of Messrs. Bramelds present difficulties to their source we have satisfaction in being able to assure the creditors that we find no reason whatever to impute to them any design to take undue advantage of their creditors. Their embarrassments have arisen mainly from the following causes— The great depression in the home trade after the ratification of the Peace in 1815, and their wish notwithstanding to employ their works to the full extent (supposing thereby to render them more profitable) drove them into the foreign markets. Their first returns from thence gave them the most flattering promise of further advantage, they were led to make greater consignments, till at length a positive loss of £22,000 was the result, as has clearly made appear to us in this investigation.

The withdrawing of so great a capital from their concern drove them to the delusive expedient of supplying that deficiency by drawing Bills of accommodation and to raise money for the payment of current wages and expenses by giving their Bills in exchange for cash notes obtained from shopkeepers and others, and which Bills they renewed from time to time at an enormous expense of commission, interest, stamps, etc. In fact they appear for the last five years to have been working upon this system of false capital borrowed at a rate of interest of from 12 to 15 per cent per annum. We feel satisfied that had it not been for the before mentioned losses and disadvantages their manufactory could now have been carried on so as to leave a considerable profit. If these works are now broken up, and the wares, fixtures and utensils disposed of to the *best immediate* advantage, one cannot but feel assured that they are of such a nature they will not fetch one half of the value at which they are now estimated.

Under this conviction it became with us a material point to consider if by any possibility they could be carried on—on behalf of the creditors. This we find impracticable without an advance of from 10 to 15,000£, an advance which under existing circumstances it would be utterly hopeless to look for. We therefore see no probable means of averting a bankruptcy.

(Signed) C. D. Faber
Wm. Newman'

Wentworth Papers: Mr. Newman's italics.

43

The grievous situation into which the pottery had fallen, shocked not only the employees directly concerned, but great numbers who would be affected by unemployment—traders, farmers, shopkeepers and the like. A petition pointing this out and signed by local creditors was sent to the Earl. This again, is worth reproduction in full—

PETITION

To the Right Honorable Earl Fitzwilliam
My Lord,

It is usual in approaching a nobleman of your Lordship's rank to set out with high pretensions, but we trust you will give us credit when we say that being your Lordship's neighbours and many of us your tenants, we know your character too well to think it necessary.

We deeply regret the occasion of our memorial by the failure of our neighbours, your Lordship's tenants at the Swinton Pottery, for the causes of which we cannot do better than beg your reference to the report laid before us at Brampton drawn up by the Provisional Assignee and your Lordship's principal agent.

It is not our business here to discuss the character of the parties, but this much we think it proper to say that however unfortunately their late affairs have turned up for your Lordship, themselves and us, we feel satisfied their past experience has qualified them to steer a safer course in future than a second time to strike upon those rocks now too well known to them.

The pottery gave direct employment to about two hundred and seventy individuals and upon these some hundreds more depended as well as a necessary weekly expenditure of cash which taken in the aggregate amounted to about £10,000 annually, flowing into circulation amongst the shopkeepers, farmers, colliers and mechanics on your Lordship's Wentworth estate.

The sudden (though not hitherto total) suspension of the works has thrown many of these poor people upon their neighbouring parishes, and much misery and distress is occasioned by it which we do not wish to press upon your Lordship's attention and give unnecessary pain to your feelings.

But we would willingly turn to a brighter part of the subject, and we humbly but earnestly entreat your Lordship to step forward on this occasion and with your accustomed beneficence lend a saving hand to preserve this old established manufactory from ruin. We are willing and anxious and do hereby wish the assignees to make an offer to your Lordship to sell the Tenant's right entire as a going concern at a reasonable price, and unless you listen to our request and kindly become the purchaser, we see no alternative but the breaking up of the whole concern which would be a great sacrifice of property and seriously injure us by the smallness to which it would reduce our dividend, and indeed much injure the property itself by exposing its best workmen and most valuable customers to the temptations which in such a state of things would be held out to them by rival manufactories with avidity.

We venture, therefore, my Lord, to hope you will add one more act of kindness to all those showered upon your neighbours in Yorkshire who would receive this blessing at your hands with gratitude, as a great part of the inhabitants are affected directly or indirectly in the prospect of a manufactory now brought into a very improved state in the quality of its productions, and which must depend upon your Lordship's liberality for its future existence.

We are, my Lord, with sincere veneration and respect,
Your Lordship's obliged and faithful servants.
(Appended are 20 signatures of persons, 17 to whom the Bramelds owe sums ranging from £13 to £900, making in all a total of about £2,000.)[1]

A cynic might well observe that the signatories too boldly identified their private interest with the public good, but there was no denying the fact of great unemployment in the neighbourhood. It may be that the Bramelds assisted in drawing up the memorial—particulars of pottery expenditure could only be given by them.—The memorialists however, spoke for many more than themselves . . .

On January 21st, 1826, after the meeting of creditors at Brampton Bull Head Inn, Mr. Newman again reported to the Earl—

"Had it not been for foreign losses, and for the great annual expenditure in keeping up a fictitious capital to supply the void occasioned by the loss of real capital abroad, this concern would now have been in a flourishing state . . .

At present the affairs of the Pottery stand thus—The Company are declared bankrupt . . . the works are to be carried on for a while for the assignees for the benefit of the creditors till the debts are proved, and the outstanding accounts got in . . ."

A hopeful note is to be perceived in Newman's final observation—

"If the Bramelds were relieved of their burden . . . by keeping to the home trade" the works would clear themselves "with advantage to his Lordship and the neighbourhood . . ."

A first meeting under bankruptcy was announced for February. When Newman wrote again to the Earl it is evident that Fitzwilliam was prepared to come forward—

[1] Wentworth Papers.

45

Feb. 8th, 1826.

"The usual meeting will take place in the course of a week or ten days for the creditors to give their sanction to the assignees to dispose of the effects by private contract, and I then apprehend I shall receive some proposition of a definite nature. I will then lose no time in waiting on your Lordship. I cannot but think that it will have a *salutary effect upon Messrs. Brameld themselves* to feel that it requires *some time* and *much consideration* on the part of your Lordship to accede to the suggestion made by Mr. Faber, which I learn from him was in effect that your Lordship should take the stock at a reduced valuation, and once more trust to them. I have no reason certainly to doubt the integrity or industry of Messrs. Brameld, but their dispositions are of too sanguine a nature".[1]

The month following—March 15th, 1826—the *Pottery Mercury* carried an announcement that "The Swinton Pottery, late in the occupation of Messrs. Brameld & Co. against whom a commission of bankruptcy has been issued and awarded" was to be let.

Meanwhile the Bramelds waited with what patience they could muster for some movement on the part of the Earl. At last having cooled their heels for a time, they were summoned on April 14th, to a conference at Wentworth House, Messrs. Maude and Newman on that occasion representing Fitzwilliam. An agreement was drawn up and particulars set out in a minute, broadly speaking as follows—

Fifteen thousand pounds was needed to carry on the Pottery. This conceded—Messrs. Brameld feel confident that the Pottery would produce an annual income of £3,000, and they have no doubt of being able to pay thereout to Earl Fitzwilliam the following sums annually—

To rent of the Pottery ...	...	...	£800
To rent of 100 acres of land ...	...		200
To interest on £15,000 cap. ...	...		750
			£1,750

After various deductions concerning obligations of assignees and stock were taken into account, the final sum to be advanced would be £10,358.

The Bramelds engaged "never to draw or accept a bill of accommodation for the purpose of raising money or obtaining credit, and never to enter upon any foreign connexion. They also engage to take stock

---

[1] In 1825 the Leeds Pottery was also in trouble. The workmen struck when the firm attempted a reduction of wages from 20 to 30%, at the same time raising the price of their goods by 50%.

46

PLATE V

a. Spill vases, mushroom, cylindrical and trumpet shapes. The large vase is 8in. high and is decorated with a painting of birds in the style of Randall. (All with puce griffin; all have gilder's *C1* mark).

b. Dessert plates. L. to R. Dark blue ground and gilt, single flower study, pink ground and gilt. (All puce griffin.)

PLATE VI

a. Basket with applied flowers, enamelled view of "*Clifton House the seat of Henry Walker, Esq.*", 12in. × 9in. (Griffin mark 45).
b. Biscuitware bust of Earl Fitzwilliam—plinth decorated in dark blue and gold. Ht. 12in. (Unmarked).
c. The Rhinoceros vase. Three panels of scenes from *Don Quixote* in enamel colours painted by John Wager Brameld. Ht. 45in. (Griffin mark 41).

annually, and to make a return thereof, and a balance sheet of their debts and credits to Mr. Maude or Mr. Newman".

They consented to "a joint bond, with a warrant of attorney upon which judgment shall be signed, so as to give the immediate power of seizing at any time, all that they may possess".[1]

Thus the Earl became the sole mortgagee with power to foreclose at will. He advanced apparently, the sum above indicated.

Backed by this guarantee, the works resumed production. In August of the same year Mr. Newman informs the Earl that he has arranged with the Doncaster bank for an advance of £4,000 in notes, and Brameld bills of exchange to be met for a further £1,000. Really, the Bramelds emerged from this shattering experience much better than anyone could have expected. The Earl's decision was in part a tribute to sound character and industry. The Pottery now entered a new lease of life. To mark the occasion, it was renamed the "Rockingham Works", a gesture for obvious reasons completely gratifying to their patron. His crest, a griffin passant, was adopted as a trade mark, and this with certain additions remained so to the end.

The story, derived from Jewitt and often recounted by commentators on the pottery (one copying another) to the effect that at a meeting in Rotherham, Earl Fitzwilliam, so impressed by the beautiful wares which Thomas Brameld there produced, decided to finance the works, is of doubtful value. The bankruptcy meeting was held (as we have seen) at Brampton Bull Head, an inn on the outskirts of Wath village; and the official bankruptcy proceedings were—according to a public announcement in the *Sheffield Iris*—terminated in two sessions at Barnsley. Throughout the estate correspondence there is no mention of a Rotherham meeting. It may be that such a meeting was held, but it is quite unlikely that a dramatic incident involving Earl Fitzwilliam took place. For years the Earl had been familiar with Brameld wares. Fine porcelain would not await a general meeting to be displayed, but would as a matter of course, at once be brought to the notice of Wentworth.

[1] Wentworth Papers.

47

CHAPTER VI

THE PHOENIX ARISES

Rockingham!

The name has commanded so much attention during the past hundred and twenty years, that it would be well to look for a moment at the man from whom the mark derives.

Charles Watson Wentworth, Second Marquis of Rockingham, who inherited the Wentworth estates through the Strafford branch of the family, was one of the most prominent Whig politicians of the eighteenth century. His lean, somewhat swarthy features, his dark calculating eyes, look out from the canvases of Reynolds and Shackleton. Spare in build, and fond of riding, his full length portrait hangs appropriately enough opposite a picture of the famous racehorse "Whistlejacket", in the room of that name at Wentworth.

He was often reproached by Edmund Burke, his secretary and conscience, for neglect of parliamentary duties; but it must be remembered that Whig leadership came not through choice, but by force of circumstance. Lecky's assessment of Rockingham on his appointment as head of the Government (1765-6) is a conditioned one. "Of ... the new Minister", he writes, "there is little to be said. A young nobleman of very large fortune and unblemished character, he had been for some time only remarkable for his passion for horse-racing ... He was selected by the Whigs as their leader, mainly on account of his property and connections, but partly on account of his conciliatory manners and high character ... He carried out a steadily liberal policy with great good sense and a perfectly single mind, and uniform courtesy to opponents ... The genius of Burke, who was his private secretary, and who was brought into parliament by his influence, has cast a flood of light upon his administration and imparted a somewhat deceptive splendour to his memory".

But Lecky, like so many historians preoccupied with literary and histrionic attributes, does Rockingham less than justice. Professor Earnshaw's finding is much more in focus. "From the moment of the installation of the Rockingham Cabinet", he writes, "the King plotted and intrigued against it. At the end of twelve months the royal conspiracy was successful, and one of the wisest, purest, and most progressive administrations of the eighteenth century was brought to an abrupt and premature termination". In 1782, for a second time, George III was compelled to call upon Rockingham and his friends, on this occasion to conclude peace with America, but it was a short-lived administration, for on July 1st at the early age of fifty-two, the Marquis

¹ Rockingham was for a long time a patron of the Doncaster Races.

died. "Full of common sense", observes J. Steven Watson in his *Reign of George the Third*. Perhaps the most fitting epitaph is that of Edmund Burke, "His virtues were his means". Recalling his general character and the elegant age in which he lived, it is not inappropriate that the highest achievement of the Swinton Pottery should perpetuate his name.

This year (1826) Earl Fitzwilliam was seventy-eight, and still philanthropic. Apart from his backing of the Pottery, he had contributed a large proportion of the £6,000 necessary to build a new church at Swinton, in which one may add, the Bramelds were down for pew holdings. He took no active part in politics. He very seldom travelled. He did however, with two coaches and six, and sixteen outriders, continue to patronise Doncaster Races.

During the racing season he entertained that popular Whig gadabout, Mr. Creevey, who has left us a thumb-nail sketch of the Earl at home. "At dinner", says Creevey, "I heard Princess Lieven say to Lord Fitzwilliam:—'Your house, my lord, or your palace, I should rather say, is the finest I have seen in England. It is both beautiful and magnificent ...' To which old Billy replied, 'It is, indeed'. She then proceeded, 'When foreigners have applied to me heretofore for information as to the houses best worth seeing in England, I have sent them to Stowe or Blenheim; but in future I shall tell them to .go down to Wentworth'. The last compliment was received by old Billy in *solemn silence!* not an atom of reply!"[1]

What did Mr. Creevey expect? The Earl, always a modest man, had said his say.

* * * *

Thus, in 1826, began at Swinton, a substantial production of porcelain, the flow increasing steadily as the years went by. As a gesture of gratitude to the Earl, and to demonstrate beyond all question the high standard of perfection he could attain—though some account must be made for its intended setting—Thomas Brameld applied himself to the manufacture of a porcelain scent-jar of gigantic size. This must have taken place not long after the Wentworth agreement, since E. Rhodes, the author of *Excursions in Yorkshire* visiting the Pottery during the latter part of 1826, saw the piece just after completion. Until the sale a few years ago, the vase was an outstanding feature of the pillared hall. Purchased by a York dealer, it was brought back to the area where it was made, and now rests in the Clifton Park Museum, Rotherham.[2]

In 1830 a beam of Royal favour shone on the Rockingham Pottery. William IV had just succeeded his brother George, and invitations were extended to quote for a ceremonial dessert service for use in the Royal

[1] Creevey Papers.

[2] In the agent's cash book for March 7th, 1827, there is payment to Bramelds for "China, etc.", of £109. 15s. 0d. This may have included (say) £100 for the scent vase.

Household. It was to cost £5,000, consisting of 144 plates and 56 larger pieces.[1] The Bramelds, competing with Derby and Worcester, submitted designs which were eventually accepted. The factory rose to the occasion; the set when complete, was encased in stout mahogany boxes (one or two of which are still in existence), and according to tradition the whole rumbled off to Windsor escorted by a squadron of cavalry.

The Bramelds hoped for great things from the special service. One can appreciate the pride with which they appended to the griffin-Rockingham inscription, "Manufacturer to the King". The attained standard could not but assist sales. Josiah Wedgwood in his day, had entertained little doubt that, "If royal or noble introduction", he said, "be as necessary to the sale of an article as real elegance and beauty, then the manufacturer if he consults his own interest, will bestow as much pains and expense too in gaining the former of these advantages, as he would in bestowing the latter". He felt that his flower-pots would sell more if they were called "Duchess of Devonshire flower-pots"; cream ware more, if called "Queen's Ware". The service which he made for Catherine the Great was artistically a failure and economically scarcely worth while, but exhibited at Greek Street and talked of throughout Europe, its association value and advertising impact were enormous. One can imagine the air of complete confidence, not to say of pride, with which John Wager Brameld would solicit orders. He represented no mean firm.

It is said that the Bramelds lost money on the Royal Service, and one may assume that they made no great profit on other orders at a similar level. None the less they were in an expansive mood. In 1832 or 1833, they bought the Kilnhurst Pottery then held by George Green, though he retained the manufactured goods, copper plates, moulds, etc. Here is proof of a strong consistent manufacture of common wares. They had a full order book.

A stock list which, though undated, must derive from the thriving days of the pottery, records—

			£	s.	d.
Best Warehouse	...	...	391	4	8
Second Warehouse	...	...	273	16	0
Clock Warehouse	...	...	366	0	0
Alleys	...	...	269	0	0
Round Warehouse	...	...	400	0	0
Sorting House ...	...	...	20	0	0
Russia	...	...	80	0	0
			1,799	0	8 [2]

[1] For later information on the service see p. 107-110.

[2] This is presumably earthenware.

50

China			£	*s.*	*d.*
Cabinet Room ...	...	...	300	0	0
Far Rooms	...	...	110	0	0
Show Room	...	...	390	0	0
White Ware Room	...	...	450	0	0
Painting Room ...	...	...	48	0	0
Burnishing Room	...	...	18	0	0
Grinding Room	...	...	10	0	0
Prism Room	...	...	70	0	0
			1,336	0	0

Over £3,000 worth of stock was being carried, and to assist sales a shop was established in York and another in Vauxhall Road, London. (Fuller detail of this latter enterprise is contained in "The Bramelds in London", *The Connoisseur*, June 1967).

An undated salary list available shows Thomas Brameld as General Manager at £750 per annum; a certain "G.G." as Cashier and Chief Clerk at £650; George Frederic Brameld as Corresponding Clerk and secretary at £100; and John Wager Brameld "Traveller and chiefly of the warehouse department" at £300. The "Chief Onlooker, or Manager of Ornamenting and Warehouse" was paid £150 per annum; Bailiff to "Assist in Painting and Gilding Department £100; Bailiff for Claymen £100; and another Bailiff for Kilnmen, £100. Hours of attendance were from 8 a.m. to 6 p.m.; dinner, 1 to 2 p.m., though one suspects this may have been a requirement for the staff only.

* * * *

A document of 1829 indicates the range of the "overlooking" personnel. Richard Shillito (of whom we shall hear more later) was to have charge of the earthenware department as general overlooker, with a man named Hulme to assist him. William Horncastle had charge of the warehouse, etc.; Mr. Wager had charge of the men on the farm; Mr. Baguley controlled all the painting and gilding department in china and enamel earthenware; John Speight the painting, etc. in earthenware biscuit work; George Liversedge was overlooker and manager of the printing department; Joseph Bullough, sorter of biscuit ware; and William Speight had charge of the Flint Mill, and also "the care and management of all gold, colours and glazes, etc., he giving them out as they may be properly wanted to use."

* * * *

The William IV service evoked real interest in royal circles. Frederica, Duchess of Cumberland, after uncertain and harassed years on the continent, settled at Kew, and there patronised the Pottery by ordering a special dessert service. John Wager Brameld, representing the firm, travelled down and submitted five pattern plates specially prepared for the purpose. He reported that Her Royal Highness was "much gratified therewith", and selecting one for style, gave the order. The Duchess was evidently a lady who knew her own mind. There were to be thirty-six plates in all—six decorated with shells, six with fruit, six with marine subjects, six having interiors—"in the style of the original" she stipulated—and six bearing landscapes, "real views", none of your idealised romantic studies! Elevated comports (*Des Assiettes Eleves*) were to be the same as those manufactured for the King, "to be shown to her as they are prepared in turns for the King to see". There were to be twelve such comports, or W.S.; two cream bowls. and two ice cellars, the whole service priced at two hundred and fifty guineas.

Where is that service now?—in Hanover, where the unpopular Duke of Cumberland, the most obnoxious of all Queen Victoria's uncles moved to become King on her accession to the throne in 1837? ("You had better go before you are pelted", advised the Duke of Wellington). We have heard of royal comports in private collections. Bearing in mind the Duke's treatment of his servants, it is not unlikely that some of his pieces mysteriously disappeared, and that the comports went this way.

In 1833, John Wager once again sends word to Swinton, this time writing from Kensington, confirming an order for a dessert service for the Duke of Sussex, who after the death of his morganatic wife, Augusta (Murray), married the Lady Cecelia Buggin, and set up a new household. Itemised as follows, the form was to be "the same as H.M.'s."

"Plate—Essex—but same size as H.M's.
4 Large Dress Plates
4 Second size Plates
8 Small Plates
4 Ice Pails (Handles à la Warwick)
4 Pine and Grape Baskets
8 Peach Baskets—say 4 mulberry and 4 pine.
4 Fruit Comports
4 Shell Comports
40 pieces—perhaps 500 guineas
6 dozens of plates
   will be 360

---

860 . . . . say £600 for 2/3".[1]

As services were also made for the King of the Belgians, the Duke of Sutherland and others of the nobility, John Wager's work as a traveller must have been varied indeed.

[1] Jewitt.

What of the artists whom the Bramelds employed?

The journeyman element was always a feature of this period, although there is ample evidence to show that in certain works a family tradition obtained—men who trained sons and nephews. Apprenticeship to the "art of painting upon china and porcelain ware" was a common condition, the binding period one of seven years. In some cases boys began working at the age of eleven, taking up apprenticeship later.

Painters passed from one pottery to another, particularly as the reputation of certain works developed. A painter might send a specimen of his work to a new place and await the response. The reputation of painters like the Steels and William Billingsley went before them, so that they had no difficulty in finding employment; though in the case of Billingsley, a rolling stone if ever there was one, tenure was likely to be uncertain.

Sometimes painters would engage for a very limited term. There is on record the curious case of a Chelsea pensioner who obtained furlough from the Hospital in order to spend a few months working at Derby. One painter stipulated for one month's clear holiday in the year. A few turned to more formal painting, and left canvases of no mean order. William Cowen, the Rockingham artist is a case in point. Some were addicted to the bottle—Edwin Steel, for example, though preoccupation with refreshment of that kind, does not seem to have impaired the quality of his work.

They were on the whole versatile workmen, capable of turning with equal ease from flower, fruit and butterfly studies, to landscapes and marine views. Their rural scenes tend to formalisation—a cottage or a classical pavilion, a vista of lake water overhung by trees, or a country seat set in its own parklands. There were times when the customer objected to the vagueness of this treatment, and requested "real views", interiors, "after the style of the original", so that guests might, when dining, be treated to a miniature picture gallery. Thus, many Rockingham plates and dishes were decorated with the noble houses of the north of England—Chatsworth and Wentworth; ruined abbeys like Roche, Norman keeps like Conisborough, castle heights like that of Scarborough, all in the romantic style of the period.

Certain painters specialised in insect, fruit or flower pieces. Collinson, two of whose expert flower paintings (seen to advantage on plates now in the Victoria and Albert Museum) bear the authentic stamp.

Payment seems to have varied according to talent, ranging from £1.5.0 to £3.0.0 per week. Contracts of service ran to increasing levels of remuneration from say, three to five years. At times a bonus was added. When John Cresswell was engaged at Swinton in 1826 on a five years contract, for the first three years he was paid at the rate of 7s. 6d. a day; the fourth year at 9s. 3d.; and the fifth year at 10s. 6d. a day.

Some painters combined brush work with an expert knowledge of the potter's art. Baguley, the gilder and painter at Swinton, carried on (though in a limited fashion) after the works closed down. Robert Allen of Lowestoft, when that pottery ceased, put up a small kiln at his own house, bought unfinished wares from the Rockingham Works, and painted and decorated these himself for sale.

The Bramelds tried to engage the best talent possible. Painters were drawn from other potteries. Thomas Steel, for example, worked both at Derby and for Herbert Minton, Stoke; Edwin Steel, the son of Thomas, had also worked at Derby. As a painter of fruit on porcelain the elder Steel had no equal. A bunch of white grapes painted from those grown in the hot-house of Earl Fitzwilliam, is considered the best specimen of his work. He painted flowers and insects also with uncommon skill.

The best known local artist employed was William Cowen, of Rotherham, who at one stage in his career was sent by Earl Fitzwilliam to study art in Italy. Depicting chiefly local scenes he exhibited in the Royal Academy sixteen times; and in 1843, published a collection of Corsican studies.

Haigh Hirstwood was with the Bramelds forty years, and when in 1839 he began business in York as a china decorator, he had worked both for the old and new dispensation. Considered as the best fly painter at Rockingham, he was capable of other skilled work, being with his two sons employed on the Royal Dessert Service. His son-in-law, William Leyland, served apprenticeship in flower painting at the pottery, and later assisted his father-in-law in the York business.

John Lucas was another artist who came from Derby, where he had learnt flower painting under his father, Daniel. He worked at Rockingham until his death in 1833, being responsible for the two plaque views of the plains of Waterloo and Chatsworth House which were exhibited in the Derby Exhibition of 1870.

George Speight was one of the most talented of the Rockingham artists. Skilled in the painting of landscapes, figures and heraldic designs, he was responsible for the well-known Strafford dish, a reproduction on porcelain of the famous Vandyke portrait of "Black Tom" dictating to his secretary. After passing from one owner to another, a member of the Fitzwilliam family saw it at the Rotherham shop of Mr. William Mason, and brought it back to Wentworth where it now remains.

Of other painters, there was John Cresswell, whose terms of employment have already been mentioned; William Eley, who modelled a fine bust of Earl Fitzwilliam; a certain Llandig (or Llandeg) painter of fruits and flowers; Ross, a painter of fruit; John Speight, (related probably to George) painter on earthenware, and Henry Tilbury, painter of landscapes and flowers.

John Randall is one about whom we have a certain amount of information. He was born at Ladywood Brossley in 1810, and died at the age of 100, thus living into the twentieth century. In 1828 he began to paint under the tuition of his uncle, T. M. Randall at Madeley. After a few years he came to Rockingham, where it is said, he stayed for a couple of years; and from thence to the Potteries and Coalport, where he stayed for forty-five years. His speciality was the painting of birds. When in 1881 his eyesight failed for ceramic painting, he turned to authorship, writing works on pottery history. A collector of minerals and fossils, he became a fellow of the Geographical Society.

Derby seems to have been the main source of supply for Rockingham artists. William Corden, landscape and figure painter; Thomas Brentnall and Collinson, fruit and flower painters, all came from Derby, as did Isaac Baguley and the two Steels. This accounts in some part for the similarity of design and colour displayed on wares from the two works.

As pendant to the above, it may be of interest to list annotations in the pattern books we have seen. The pattern number is given with a directive to the painters—

No.

684 "Gold hoops to match French cape (?) sent by Cocker from Derby".
916 "Russell's birds flying".
688 "Llandeg's blackberry border".
671 "Plants by Mr. Hoyland".
681 "Llandeg's leaf and hazel blossom".
640 "A bunch of fruit in centre by James Ross".
914 "1 small flower by Steel".

several "Flowers by girls", or "painting by women".
789 "Centre by Speight".
790 "Leyland's Sprigs".
847 "Oval Shields, plants by Kent".

*   *   *   *

At one time or another artists worked in and about Wentworth House. The Vandyke copy has been mentioned, and the fruit painted by Thomas Steel. In 1826, Haigh Hirstwood was lengthily engaged making copies for use on Rockingham china of Lady Milton's collection of "insects" (moths, butterflies, etc.) numbering over 500. This would form a separate pattern book of its own. Rare plants were copied from the gardens and painted on the Rhinoceros vase.

Further afield, small water colour sketches were made on the spot. Clifton House, Clifton Park (displayed on wares), would certainly be so sketched. The present writers have in their possession a small water colour of Roche Abbey, almost certainly the work of William Cowen.

Such were the men who, along with girl assistants, were responsible for the decoration of the fine porcelain which emanated from the Rockingham Pottery from 1826 to 1842.

Note—
   For easy reference the names of all known Rockingham artists and workpeople are printed in *italics* in the Index.

CHAPTER VII

THE GILDED YEARS

One article of the 1826 agreement was that a balance sheet of trading should be submitted to Wentworth each year. These were for a time favourable, making good the promise made by the Bramelds on re-habilitation—

1827 (Dec. 31st) the pottery showed a balance of £1537 17 3
1829 (Feb. 28th)   „   „   „   £1043 13 2
1830 (Apr. 3rd)   „   „   „   £1121 8 2
1831 (Oct. 3rd)   „   „   „ (a loss) £996 2 8

In 1831, however, bad debts amounted to £1,085.15.3, as against £871.6.7 in 1830.

No balance sheets seem to be available after 1831.

But general, imponderable factors now pressed upon them. Trading competition the Bramelds took for granted; this could be assessed and reckoned with; but what in the early thirties, were they to do with the situation created by the agitation for Parliamentary Reform, and concurrently, the widespread epidemic of cholera? "The great topic now in London", wrote Macaulay to his sister at this time, "is not as perhaps you fancy, Reform, but Cholera. There is a great panic; as great a panic as I remember, particularly in the City. Rice shakes his head and says that this is the most serious thing which has happened in his time, and assuredly if the disease were to rage in London as it has lately raged in Riga, it would be difficult to imagine anything more horrible".

Cholera spread rapidly throughout the country. In Rotherham, the market town nearest the pottery, corpses were being carried in long wicker baskets to a burial ground set apart off Doncaster Road, the churchyard being closed to the victims. Streets were isolated; fast days and prayer meetings held. As people were afraid to make contact with their fellows, trade languished, and the pottery began to feel the pinch, although the epidemic is not the sole subject for complaint in the letter which follows. The Bramelds were in financial trouble again. Mr. Newman (Mr. Bowns having either died or retired) had apparently written in August reminding the Bramelds that certain sums were due to Wentworth, and Thomas Brameld replied—

W. Newman, Esq.   Rockingham Works, 28th Aug., 1832.
Sir!
      We were favor'd with your letter of the 22nd. and exceedingly regret that we are not able to pay as we ought to do. We assure you that everything is done that we possibly can by every means

¹ Wentworth Papers.

57

in our power; but such has been the dreadful state of everything connected with business for the last eighteen months from political agitation and the effects of the awful malady now raging, and so severely too in many places and parts where our business lays—as London, the Eastern Coast generally and the whole of Scotland—that all efforts and plans have failed to produce sufficient current means.

In such circumstances we are under the necessity—and it is indeed truly painful to us—of saying that we find the amount of capital is not adequate for the welfare of the concern, and that as the struggles that we have been making to produce the desired effect have only tended to be injurious, we think it better to ask your kind permission for our T. Brameld to solicit the favour of an interview with My Lord Milton that he may himself explain our case to his Lordship.

Altho, we cannot do good as we ought to do, from not having as much disposable means as our rivals in the business, yet we are very confident that the concern has not lost anything; even the loss which appeared at last balance was only the consequence of sacrifices made on a part of the old and bad stock, a good deal of which yet remains, for it has been hopeless to expect to dispose of it.

The way we have been working the last two years is however calculated for safety that all we have the means of getting up is available in the market, and there is no doubt whatever of a profitable result henceforth if we can go on so as to fully employ the works. Although we have seldom done more than half, and never more than two thirds, not having had the means in our power of going beyond it. We ought to manufacture to the extent of £400 a week—or £20,000 a year—and we believe the proper interest of the works here cannot be secured without the capital employed is equal to the annual production of goods. Our shop at York (with the exception of the present suspension of business from the Pestilence) is a very good concern and furnishes us with great help in the weekly receipt of ready moneys, but it takes an extra capital of about £2,000. The London wholesale place in Vauxhall Road lost money at first, but it is now become so far established as to do enough to pay its way (except of late from the two great and important causes of stagnation), and we are *quite sure* that it is capable of being a lucrative concern now. Indeed, had it not been for the goods vended by it, the works would not in Earthenware have been more than *one quarter*, for the Country Journies which used to amount to 8, 9, or 10,000£ a year, have not of late reached more than about 3,000 to 4,000£, and the ready money sales at home which used to be about £40 a week, have lately not been £5 a week.

The London concern requires a capital of 6 to 7,000£, but that is not all *extra* on the general capital, as a portion—say half of it—is supplied from the stock here which is by the supplies to London, constantly kept lower than it would otherwise be. The retale (*sic*) part of the London trade is gradually on the increase, although it has not yet done much good for want of perhaps a good *Shop*. The stock in it is part of the above 6 to 7,000£ and does not probably exceed a 1,000£ because it is fed regularly from the Warehouse, and on that account can be kept low.

It appears to us that goods now are and are likely to be, more wanted, and as our present new patterns are very good, our J. W. Brameld who is now in Scotland, is obtaining better orders. Those also on the English Journey are better than this time last year, so that if we could pay wages regularly between now and the end of the current year, we can pledge ourselves to make you *monthly payments,* commencing on January next of *one hundred and fifty pounds each.*

Now Thomas Brameld arrives at the crucial point of his long explanatory letter—

I have also to pay the amount due to Messrs. Cooke & Co. —about 750£, to the Assignees about 500£, and coal accounts to New Parkgate and Low Wood about £250. What we otherwise owe, and all current expenses for materials etc. will be fully covered by the income between now and the end of the year, so that if we are favoured by my Lord Milton with the means of paying as above, the concern will be free from all other debt at the end of the year, and we shall have the means of keeping it so, and of paying our way regularly as we know very well that we can manufacture as good an article for the market as any other house, and by means of reduced expenditure in everything we can afford to sell at market prices and ensure business.

The service we are preparing for the King will now be completed with an outlay of from 5 to 700£, and when we are paid for it, we can pay you an extra sum of £2,000. When this service and that for the Duchess of Cumberland are delivered, we confidently anticipate a considerable increase in our retale trade in general, and particularly in London.

We are aware that this is an important communication to make to you, and the writer's feelings have been excessively harassed before he could make resolution to set about it, but the nature of circumstances requires us to do it, and we can only trust to the kind indulgence of my Lord Milton and yourself to allow it the most favourable attention, and to afford us an opportunity of explanation on whatever points his Lordship may wish.

We have written more at length because the nervous anxiety of the writer is so great that he could not express himself personally; yet he trusts that if my Lord Milton kindly allows him a private interview he can give him any explanation he may require, and which he is anxious to have the opportunity of doing.

We are, Sir / very respectfully
Your most obliged Servt
For Self and Brothers,
Thomas Brameld.[1]

Thomas must have received a disappointing reply from Lord Milton, who, on the advanced age of his father, had assumed estate direction. Matters had now become desperate, for in his next letter, Brameld makes a direct request for weekly subsidies to meet wages.

To Lord Milton   Rockingham Works, 8th Sept., 1832.

My Lord,
From a letter I received this morning from Mr. Newman my grief and distress is very great in learning that your Lordship feels unwilling to afford us assistance.

It is true that we ought to have no need of it now after all the help and kindness we have experienced from your Lordship, but there are circumstances, my Lord, besides the important and very oppressive ones I mentioned to Mr. Newman which have been the main cause of producing our difficulties; and the present untoward state of business has complicated the measure of them, and set us so fast, that we really do not know what is best to be done for want of present means.

These points I will endeavour to explain as well as I can to your Lordship if you will be good enough to favour me with an interview for an hour; and when your Lordship has heard my explanation if you can have confidence in us so far as kindly to assist us with a loan of £2,000[2] until we can finish and get paid for His Majesty's service we will then repay it, and I have full confidence in being able ultimately to satisfy your Lordship's wishes; for every letter I receive from my brother Wager in Scotland is more favourable in orders—and in proof of the ground our goods are gaining in character, as well as more proof of amendment in the times.

[1] Wentworth Papers.

[2] In weekly sums of £125 each for the next sixteen weeks from this time.

I propose going to Wentworth on Monday morning with this letter, and there wait upon your Lordship's leisure for allowing me the honour of an interview.

Yours, etc., etc.,

T. Brameld.'

Thomas Brameld must have managed an interview that fateful morning, for after listening to his persuasive tongue, Lord Milton so far relented, as to ask (it would seem) for some detailed proof of the claim to reviving trade. The upshot was another letter to the agent, setting out particulars of Scottish and East Anglian prospects—

To William Newman   Rockingham Works, 20th Sept., 1832.

Sir,

I am sorry I have not been able to furnish you with the accounts of the Scotch journey. I have now received from my brother Wager from Glasgow the separate calculation of each customer's order—as taken—and the difference is seen between the two journeys (1832 and 1833) (*sic*) to be nearly 3 to 1 in favour of the present and probably have been ful! 4 if not 5 to 1 had not Glasgow and the neighbourhood been so severely injured, and again *this* is not the season for the most orders. The Spring journies (*sic*)—if all is in regular course—are generally *one third* better than these for orders.

I am not able to give the separate names and accounts of the Norfolk journey, but Spring was £736 and the present £650— this we consider an improvement—we hardly hoped for more than £400 or £450. In some towns the cholera was so severe not an order was taken. The young man who travels for us in Norfolk says in his letters that he thinks the shopkeepers and people generally are in better spirits and hope to do more largely next Spring. The extreme deficiency of the circulating medium keeps them constantly so fast that they dare not order so much as they would otherwise. The Norfolk journey used to be 2 and 3,000£ a few years ago on the same ground as above. During the late war and a few years after it was about £4,000. We do not despair to seeing it improved to something like it once was.

Yours, etc., etc.,

Thomas Brameld.

Attached to the sheet was John Wager's list setting out Scottish orders from various towns, totalling—Spring, 1832, £404.12.3*d.;* Autumn, 1832, £1,117.0.0*d.*'

Wentworth Papers.

61

The situation had become so serious that John Wager cut short his journeying and hurried back to the Pottery. From thence at once he wrote to Lord Milton—

27th September, 1832.

My Lord!

I arrived home last evening from Liverpool, and learning from my brother that your Lordship expressed a wish to see a comparative statement of my last four journeys, I have written one out, and beg to enclose it for your Lordship's inspection.

Part of my journey is yet unfinished, which I hope will increase the account considerably, but I came over for a day or two finding my brother in so anxious a state of feeling.

I have the honour to be, my Lord,
With much respect for brother and self.
Your Lordship's
Most obliged and humble servant
J. W. Brameld.[1]

The attached sheet is interesting not only as a transcript of Wager's places of call, but of certain annotations having their own significance. He takes £45.0.0 worth of orders in Newcastle, and comments "80 cases of cholera reported in Newcastle the day J.W.B. was there, or else orders probably good". He passed on to Alnwick, Berwick, Dunfermline, Dundee, Montrose, Arbroath, Perth, Edinburgh, Leith, Peebles. Stirling and Glasgow successively. Of Glasgow he remarks, "Traders ruined on account of Cholera".

From Glasgow he moved to Paisley, Kilmarnock, Dumfries, Carlisle, Penrith, Kendal, Lancaster, Liverpool, Manchester and Buxton. Certain old customers he writes down simply as "failed", but whether in business, or in his own ability to secure an order, is by no means clear. Against the name of one shop he writes, "Just in time", whatever that may mean.

His final note runs: "The greatest quantity of goods are sold generally on the Spring Journey, but for nearly twelve months past the sad ravages of Cholera, the great alarm it produced, and the unsettled state of men's minds in respect of politics (especially in Scotland) caused a great suspension of business. The alarm seems now wearing off, chiefly I think for the complaint being more familiarised to people, and times are a shade better. Besides which our last new shapes and quality of improved earthenware are highly approved of and have helped sales much.   J.W.B.

*   *   *   *

This sanguine report produced the desired effect, for in the Agent's Account Book for 1832 is an entry, "Sundry Sums for the purpose of enabling Messrs. Brameld to pay their workmen"—

[1] Wentworth Papers.

62

PLATE VII

a. Rockingham figures. L. to R. *"Paysanne du Canton de Zurich"*. Ht.
7in. (Griffin *impressed*, No. 18); *"Simon Pengander"*. Ht. 6½in. (No. 7
impressed); *"Paysan du Canton de Zurich"*. Ht. 7in. (Griffin *impressed*,
No. 53).
b. (*Below left*) Rococo vase (pot-pourri) and cover. Ht. 11in. (Puce griffin).
c. (*Below right*) Porcelain jug. Green ground and gilt. Enamel flower painting. Ht. 8in. (Puce griffin).

PLATE VIII

a. Circular decorative basket, cross-twigs handles, applied coloured flowers. Ht. 3in. (Puce griffin *C*1 3); Scent bottle and stopper with applied coloured flowers. Ht. 4½in. (Puce griffin); Posy bowl, the handle is a later addition, uncoloured applied flowers on the rim, flower painting all round the base. Total height 3½in. (Puce griffin).

b. Spill vase—strawberry plant enamel decoration. Ht. 3½in. (Red griffin, *C*1 11); Candleholder in the form of a flower. Ht. 2in. Diam. 4½in. (Puce griffin); Circular inkstand dark pink ground and gold. Ht. 2in. (Red griffin, *C*1 6).

	£		£
Sept. 29th	250	Nov. 17th	130
Oct. 6th	100	„ 24th	130
„ 13th	150	Dec. 1st	130
„ 20th	130	„ 8th	130
Nov. 3rd	130	„ 15th	130
„ 10th	130	„ 22nd	130
„ 16th	150	„ 29th	130

Thus, week by week, a total of £1,950 was advanced.[1] It will be noted that these payments ceased at the year end. In the new year, one presumes, the Royal service was paid for, and the Bramelds moved into calmer waters.

[1] Wentworth Papers.

CHAPTER VIII

ECLIPSE AND DECLINE

In 1833, Lord Milton succeeded his father as the 3rd Earl Fitzwilliam. The new Earl had come far since the day on the hustings at York when he had been derided on account of his youth by the Hon. Henry Lascelles. Handed a whip and top by his Tory opponent, with quick wit, he had flung the top into the crowd, and handed back the whip with the observation that it would serve well for lashing Harewood's West Indian slaves! The crowd rose to the quip, for all present were aware of the Lascelles rich sugar interests.

He was now a middle-aged man of forty-seven, a seasoned politician in the liberal tradition of his father. Active enough in the House of Commons, he had once aroused the ire of William Cobbett being the subject of a *Political Register* "open letter" in which not only had his Lordship's principles been brought into question, but his faulty grammar also! Opposed to radical parliamentary reform, he had at last been brought round to enthusiastic support for the more limited measure of 1832. Sydney Smith, who voted for him at one election, described him as "one of the most ungainly young men" that he had ever seen. A year after Milton became Earl, Creevey with whom he had long sat and voted in the Commons, observed that he was due to take dinner with "Praise God Barebones Fitzwilliam". To that inveterate social and political gossip the father had always been "Old Billy". One gathers that in character and temperament, the new Earl had less of geniality; was much more earnest and severe than his predecessor.

For years, during the advanced age and declining health of his father the new Earl had become familiar with—and to a large extent controlled —estate business. His relations with the Bramelds had always been friendly—we have seen how he responded to their request for a loan in '32—but he was at one remove from the old association; one feels personally withdrawn.

For the time being the Pottery appeared to be on an even keel, indeed full set for prosperity. The ornate dinner and dessert services had brought their reputation high. And this level was maintained by a great variety of specially decorated wares. With all this they produced a large flow of tea and coffee services and of course many other varieties.

During this period Rockingham wares left the country and were sold abroad. On Sept. 20th 1832, the precise day upon which Thomas Brameld furnished Mr. Newman with details of recent orders secured by John Wager, the *Montreal Gazette* carried the following announcement: "ELEGANT CHINA AND EARTHENWARE;—On WEDNESDAY next the 26th instant, at the OLD DISTILLERY STORES:—22 packages of China Tea, Coffee, Breakfast, Dessert, and Supper Setts, of the ROCKINGHAM,

WORCESTER, and DERBY manufactories, New Dresden and fancy China Jugs, in setts, Earthenware . . . . . Sale at ONE o'clock. ADAM L. MAC-NIDER. Sept. 20".

We assume that a factor had purchased a consignment of wares, probably from the Vauxhall Road shop, and shipped them, with others, for sale across the Atlantic.

And yet the next few years were those of financial declension. It may be that some of their noble customers were tardy in payment, and certainly no blame could be laid at this period to foreign losses; by the terms of their 1826 agreement such trade was out. A tenuous local tradition maintains that the Bramelds spent time and labour on elaborate wares from which they were unable to recoup themselves financially. This may well be so, for such information would leak out among the workmen, some of whose descendants still live in the district.

Then their business in Scotland, East Anglia and London, presupposed difficulty of communication. Did the Bramelds have to wait from one journey to the next for repayment? Bad debts had become a feature of their balance sheet. Finding themselves in financial difficulty, they were unable to borrow. There is no sign that in this sense they ever approached the Earl again. In view of the last warning, they felt no doubt, that he had had enough. By the terms of the 1826 agreement they were prevented from borrowing elsewhere, from banks or in any manner whatsoever. Thus when "the circulating medium" became scarce, they were reduced to running the Pottery on a hand-to-mouth basis. From one place or another in the record, we gather too that they were most reluctant to reduce staff, largely because once lost, good workmen, they felt, would never return.

The hand-to-mouth basis is displayed in a communication from Benjamin Biron, agent for the Elsecar pit, who, on February 1st, 1837, writes laying down conditions on which the Pottery is to be supplied with coal—

> "I . . . have no objections to your payments been (*sic*) made weekly, provided they are made in cash and punctually made. I will give directions for your account to be made up to Friday night each week, and shall expect a remittance from you every Monday morning."[1]

There can be no mistaking the bearing of that note—payment on the nail, when it must be remembered, hard coal was only 5s. 6d. a ton, and soft coal, 4s. 6d.

Their difficulties increased. No firm tends to preserve dunning letters, and one may safely conclude that the kiln fires in their time consumed many such unwelcome papers; indeed, the Brameld industrial documents amount to next to nothing. Mr. William Mason relates that

Wentworth Papers.

65

on one occasion he read a letter from the Bramelds to a customer asking for the account to be paid in guineas as they wished to melt these down for the decoration of wares.

When Queen Victoria ascended the throne, bearing in mind the ornate service they had manufactured for her uncle, they made a proposal whereby the set, could so to speak be brought up to date by substituting a new set of plates. The cost, they reckoned, would not run to more than £1,700, but the offer was rejected.

One means of reviving their business, they felt, during this awkward period, lay in manufacturing something quite novel, quite new. Furniture then was generally made of rosewood or mahogany. Four-poster beds were still in use, as one can see from illustrations to the first editions of Dickens' novels. Why not porcelain bed-posts, curtain rails, and the like? In 1838, a certain Mr. Dale, from Staffordshire, approached them with an invention to this end, and quickly they concluded an agreement not only to manufacture the objects of Mr. Dale's fancy, but to find employment for the inventor as well. The terms ran—

"Brameld and Co. agree to buy from Mr. Wm. Dale of Shelton, his interest in a certain invention he has now in the Patent Office in London for the manufacture of China, Ironstone China or Earthenware Pillars, Columns or Rails, &c., for Bed-posts, Window-Heads, &c., &c., and for obtaining the Patent right of which he has entered a Caveat and taken other preliminary steps.

Brameld & Co. agree to employ the said Wm. Dale in the manufacture of them under the Patent, and also in the general management of the China Clay department at the Rockingham Works for seven years . . . at a yearly salary of eighty pounds.[1]

There were further conditions governing a yearly premium conditional on sales, and for annulment in case of failure to obtain patent rights. These last however, were obtained, and the document enrolled on September 10th, 1838.

Certain bed-posts and rails were indeed manufactured at Swinton, but alas! the heyday of the four-poster bed had gone. Brass and iron bedsteads were coming in, and rapidly becoming fashionable. Mr. William Dale's sojourn at the factory cannot have lasted long.

The fate of Dame Troth Mallory's effigy may be mentioned here. This lady, a benefactress of the poor of Rotherham, Rawmarsh and Ecclesfield, bequeathed in the early part of the seventeenth century, charities which are still employed for their original purpose. Her local association was with Aldwarke Hall, the residence of her first husband, Sir Godfrey Fuljambe (later she married Sir John Mallory). After her death an alabaster memorial figure was placed in Rawmarsh Church, but when this building in a great state of disrepair was pulled down in

[1] Jewitt.

1838, the figure (also we may take it, somewhat the worse for wear) was sold as a job lot to the Rockingham Pottery for a pound. So away they trundled poor decrepit Dame Mallory up the long hill to the works, there to process cups and saucers, plates and dishes—a sad utilitarian fate for the relic of one so gracious and dignified!

*　　*　　*　　*

The mood of England in 1839 was uneasy, sullen, bioken at times by sharp explosions of anger. Poverty was widespread, and the Chartists who claimed that the working classes had been cheated of franchise rights by the 1832 Reform Bill, were everywhere active. We read of much agitation among the Staffordshire potters, mass meetings and the like. South Yorkshire, and Sheffield in particular, seethed with discontent.

Fortunately the General in command of the Northern District was the humane, comprehending, Sir Charles James Napier, who handled the situation with consummate skill. Although heavily pressed to act militarily by alarmed manufacturers and landowners, he held his hand, determined that magistrates should not interfere with public demonstrations, or be supported by the troops under his command, unless peace was actually broken. Sometimes it was, but such outbursts were sporadic and speedily quelled. Infrequent lulls in the storm were equally disturbing. "Everything is quiet", he wrote to Lord Fitzroy, "but I confess I don't feel in its continuence beyond a couple of months. There are many mischievous persons at work, who I fear, only wait for dark nights".

It is interesting to note that the only record of trouble with the workpeople in Bramelds employment falls within this period. Though there is no hint of political disaffection in the letter from R. Shillito to Thomas Brameld which follows, it is hard otherwise to account for the malaise described in a firm so long established and supervised by a reasonable manager living on the spot. The letter was undoubtedly, a cry from the heart—

> From R. Shillito, General Overlooker, to T. Brameld.
> Rockingham Works, 6th September, 1839.
> Sir,
> Excuse the liberty I now take of addressing a few lines to you with respect to our mode of working.
> One half of the men are doing little or nothing, and yet have money to spend and get drunk with (*it*). I fear there is something very seriously wrong amongst us which ought not to be. In some of the wages bills, etc. for instance, Joseph Oxley's wages this

Life of Sir Charles James Napier, Vol. II, Sir W. Napier. It is significant that Earl Fitzwilliam was not among those who badgered Napier for military support.

week (*are*) as totalled, £1.17.6—Joseph Morton, £1.10.0 and today (*they are*) drinking and taken one of the apprentices, and with him Wm. Ely James—the above (*sums*) on account as we have no kiln this week. Charles Malton is not working half his time, and his regular wages in the bills (*are*) more than he earns considerably. It matters not what work I want doing, I cannot depend on him, besides doing his work wretchedly bad.

John Ely left us about a fortnight or three weeks ago, and (*I*) told Joseph Hoyland not to pay him any more wages as he had left without any notice after been (*being*) taken on out of pity's sake the last time. He has had regular wages put in and not earned four shillings a week since he was taken back. This week he has 12/- in the bill. Wm. Barton I am informed was in debt when he left us, and had wages put in the bill 14 or 16 weeks after he had left the works. If such things be allowed, no wonder you are in such straights . . .

These are only a few specimens amongst many. My life is quite miserable to see such villany (*sic*) and impression (*sic*). For the last 2 or 3 months I have been out of all manner of patience to see the little work done for the money in many instances. I have been applied to for work both by children and men, and given preference to the apprentices. They have applied to others and have been set on, and as often as not (*set*) theirselves on so that their wages have actually been paid for doing nothing. I have not the least doubt if I had all under my care and supported by you, sir, of saving at least five or six pounds a week in the hovels.   There is not one half work done for the wages. Over biscuit which we formerly set in two days work, two men now takes five or six the same time.

> Your humble servant,
> R. Shillito.'

This is by any assessment an extraordinary letter. It reveals in the once thriving organisation, a loss of control, a falling apart at the centre. Men had left, some drawing wages even in absence; of those who remained, drunkenness, and reluctance for work. Where were the three partners in all this? Incapacitated by illness, or all of them engaged on desperate journeys to secure both orders and cash? This year (1839) the Bramelds sold the Kilnhurst Pottery which they had held as a subsidiary for seven years, to the Twigg Brothers, who marked the occasion by producing a dish having a transfer picture of the Swinton Pottery as it then stood, the only general view now in existence.

The writing was on the wall. In spite of that—because of it—the Bramelds were willing to consider new ventures. Why not the exploita-

Sheffield Reference, "Rockingham Pottery".

tion of a completely new region? A Mr. Dillwyn had taken over the "Glamorgan Pottery", Swansea, and in 1840 negotiations were started with the object of collaboration with the Bramelds. Concerning this, Jewitt prints an interesting letter from the Swansea side—

"Gentlemen,—I am altogether unacquainted with the china manufacture and should therefore decline any partnership in one. I have, however, no doubt that china may be manufactured very profitably in Swansea, and should rejoice to see a manufacture established here. I am also convinced that a china and earthenware factory might very materially assist each other in many ways. On these accounts I have made an arrangement, at some inconvenience to myself by which I shall be enabled to let you the Glamorgan Pottery, which I should think was in every way well calculated for a china work. I am ready also to let the premises to you on lower terms than I should have expected from any other party.

The terms I would let them upon to you would be £300 per annum, with a stipulation on your part that nothing but china of the best transparent body should be manufactured upon them.

Should you think this offer worth your consideration, if one of your firm will come down, I shall be happy to show him everything in my power.

I remain, Gentlemen,
Yours very truly,
L. L. Dillwyn.[1]

Messrs. Brameld & Co.,
Near Rotherham.

This letter bears a pencilled note by Mr. Brameld, "Too high unless a good mill with it".

Thus negotiations fell through. The Bramelds must have proposed partnership hoping that if Mr. Dillwyn provided the capital, they for their part, would contribute their manufacturing skill.

*   *   *   *

A year—which must have been one of harassed endeavour—passed. At last, in December, 1841, the blow fell, though one must assume that for some time they had been forewarned. They received a document from the Estate Office—

"To Messrs. Thomas Brameld, George Frederic Brameld, and John Wager Brameld—

Take notice, that I have this day and by the order and for the use of Earl Fitzwilliam, your landlord, taken and distrained the several stock in trade, fixtures, etc., etc. . . secured for a distress

[1] Jewitt.

for the sum of four thousand and five hundred pounds for rent
and arrears owing from you to the said Earl Fitzwilliam".

Dated 21st December, 1841.

Edward Lancaster, Bailiff to the

said Earl Fitzwilliam.[1]

The order (as we have suggested) could not have been unexpected.
For years they had been unable to pay rent, and the lengthy patience
of Wentworth House had become exhausted.

So after almost a hundred years of active life the pottery closed down.
For some months accounting, and presumably the selling of standing
stock took place. And then—silence. After an appreciable time had
passed Thomas Brameld, who still held to the inch, made a final plea
to recommence business. Already he had been allowed to work the
Flint Mill, and heartened by this limited concession, decided to press
the larger claim. The letter he now writes is not without pathos. He
would, he says, manufacture on a modest scale, making only goods for
actual orders, etc. But let the letter speak for itself—

To Earl Fitzwilliam: The Cottage, 29th Novr., 1842.
My Lord,

I feel more than usual delicacy and hesitation addressing
your Lordship, and should not now pressume to do so but for a
report current around us that the works are intended to be re-
commenced—and therefore it is that I write, and I venture to
hope that your Lordship will do me and my brother Frederic
the favour to receive this kindly and take our humble request
into your indulgent consideration.

Before I proceed further I wish to express my sincere thanks
to your Lordship for kindly consenting to our request to occupy
the Flint Mill.

The purpose of our further respectful wishes, is to be allowed
the chance of carrying on our own favourite trade, the manufacture of China, and that you will kindly let us have the whole
of the works, and the use of the fixtures, models and other
utensils, for in such case we feel confidently that we can find
friends in the form of partners, or otherwise to furnish us with
the money we should consider necessary to enable us to go on in
the circumscribed way we have laid down to ourselves, without
ever thinking of asking pecuniary aid from your Lordship on
account of the manufactory. I name the whole of the works,
because altho' we should only carry on the China, yet as many of
the Earthenware Forms, and Engravings are also occasionally
used for China, and would be frequently wanted for matching

[1] Wentworth Papers.

up sets for parties who have purchased of us; it would tend to the better success of our operations to have the whole—and I may truly say we could but ill succeed without them.

We are desirous of proceeding very cautiously, being fully bent on only making goods for actual orders: and we shall wish to take time for every necessary arrangement to be properly made ere we commence; for we intend at first to limit it to the least establishment of people with which any regular business can be carried on. Our plan will be to let alone all articles save those of most common use and demand, as Tea and Breakfast Ware, and a few common Desserts. To make *some* of the old superior sort of China, as hitherto, but also to introduce from our Formula a Common and cheaper form of China at such prices as will be likely to ensure a free sale. We purpose doing all our business ourselves, without a clerk or any expensive managers.

I would here wish respectfully to suggest to your Lordship that I feel no little anxiety to be allowed myself to use the models which have cost me great care and attentive anxiety to produce, rather than they should be used by another party.

We respectfully suggest to be allowed to point out a considerable number of the old ruinous and useless buildings as desirable to be taken down. The rest we think it probable may be used to advantage ere long, and although we do not wish to ask for any expenditure of money which can be avoided yet we venture to hope that your Lordship will kindly allow us to have the useful part put into decent repair without any fresh erections until we can prove that we have good grounds to ask the favour of such alterations as will make the premises more suitable and convenient. But, at present, one thing is very important—say to have the fence wall around the Works made complete out of the materials of the old buildings to be pulled down—for that we have always been most grievously robbed to a very serious extent there is no doubt whatsoever.

There is not any doubt but profits may be made upon the manufacture of China, and indeed have been by us, but unfortunately they have merged in, and been swallowed up by, the general and sweeping expenses of the bad system we have so long laboured under.

The circumstances of the works being at a distance from the navigation is of very much less importance in the manufacture of China than earthenware, and our China really sells so well to the Trade, in fact *has such a preference in the market* that the quantity which could be produced would be sure to meet with a ready sale. This is no fancied estimate, but founded on the fact that we have always had great difficulty to produce *sufficient for*

71

our orders, and that, had the works been capable of turning out more, we could readily have disposed of it to safe people. This is quite in accordance with our own experience in London, for at Piccadilly we could always sell our own Tea, Breakfast and Dessert China much more readily than that we had from four or five other manufactories. My son finds it the case now, and is distressed because we cannot supply him with the articles so much wanted.

> I have the honour to be, on the part of myself and
> my brother Frederic, your Lordship's
> most grateful and obedient humble servant,
> Thomas Brameld.[1]

To the Rt. Hon:
The Earl Fitzwilliam.

From the foregoing certain facts emerge. Quite apart from the continued optimism of Thomas Brameld, and his faith in the Swinton product, it will be seen that now he speaks only for George Frederic and himself. John Wager has evidently gone to start his new career in London. Then the writer mentions his own son at one of their shops. This was John Thomas, the second son, aged twenty-three. For his London career see *The Connoisseur*, June, 1967.

The general appearance of the pottery at this stage must have been one of pronounced dilapidation. Thomas mentions "a considerable number of the old ruinous and useless buildings" in need of demolition. After all, under the Brameld regime alone, the pottery had been running for thirty-five years. A great deal of money would be needed to make the place ship-shape again.

The Earl and his Agent certainly realised this, for nothing came of the letter. Fitzwilliam did, however, consent to Thomas Brameld carrying on the Flint Mill, and must have inquired how much this would cost. Here is Thomas Brameld's reply—

To William Newman   16th December, 1842.
Dear Sir,

Agreeable with your directions I now beg to hand you an estimate of the capital necessary to carry on the Flint Mill. I have not done it as soon as you wished, for I have had great hesitation—and repeated calculations—to try to reduce it the most possible; for I have often known us to have as much as from 1200 to even 1500 or 1600£ in the mill department. And as it is of so very material importance to us, I feel a proportionate degree of timidity in making the statements—but you kindly said you wished me to be candid, and therefore it is that I very respectfully state the lowest sum which I truly believe will enable

[1] Wentworth Papers.

72

us to be in a situation to supply the customers—by the greatest good management and care.

Before I proceed on the subject of the yard wall I have a duty to perform in justice to decency and the reasonable comfort of an excellent servant, Samuel Parker. He has four sons and five daughters, nearly all young men and women, and only *two* bedrooms for himself and his wife and all the nine young persons. For several years I have wished to let him have some extra conveniences, and as I now think there will be, with your kind permission, an excellent chance to do it. I have very carefully gone into calculations and I find that if you will allow me £100 in money I can take down the requisite old dilapidated buildings, selling the spare part of them further towards the cost, and will then add the needful to Samuel's house, build the yard wall and remove all the rubbish out of the premises. I have no object of gain in this as I trust you will think from the sum of £100 being all I solicit in money both for Samuel's accommodation and securing the premises from thieves; and I shall feel thankful if I can have the privilege of doing this myself, as I feel confident it cannot be done by anybody else for so small an expenditure.

I am, Dear Sir,
Very respectfully,
Your obliged servant,
Thomas Brameld.

W. Newman, Esq.

Enclosure—Estimate of Capital to carry on the Flint Mill, £837.3.4*d*. Towards this Brameld has stocks amounting to £465.0.0*d*. He asks for £372.3.4*d*.[1]

* * * *

Inexorably, the once thriving concern moved to its close. On January 7th, 1843, a notice appeared in the advertisement columns of the *Sheffield and Rotherham Independent* announcing the sale of "the whole of the extensive stock at the Works at *Very Reduced Prices*—Wholesale and Retail Dealers may be supplied, as well as private families".

From this it would appear that the Bramelds had been conceded a respite in which to recoup on sales what they could; in effect a three months term of grace, for on April 8th, a further notice appeared—

Sale by Mr. Lancaster.

———

ROCKINGHAM WORKS
extensive sale of
CHINA, EARTHENWARE, Biscuit Ware
and other effects at Messrs.
BRAMELDS MANUFACTORY, SWINTON

Wentworth Papers.

Mr. Lancaster respectfully announces that he is directed
to SELL BY AUCTION, without reserve, on Monday, Tues-
day and Thursday, the 1st, 2nd and 4th days of May, 1843
(and on the following day Friday, if necessary) the valuable
stock of China, Earthenware, and Biscuit Ware, the particulars of which will appear in next week's paper.

Thus, the following week Mr. Lancaster set out in full the stock
to be sold—

"The valuable STOCK OF CHINA which embraces Dinner
and Dessert Services, Breakfast, Tea and Coffee Equipages;
250 dozen of China plates and dishes; 300 dozen of tea
and breakfast cups and saucers, Milk Jugs, Slop and Sugar
Bowls, Cream Ewers, Water Ewers, Jugs, etc.; a variety of
Scent Jars, Vases, and other decorative articles, including
some Beautifully finished Cabinet specimens.

The EARTHENWARE which is very extensive comprehends
a general assortment of Table Ware, including 750 dozen
in various patterns of Dishes, Plates, Drainers, Vegetable
dishes, Sauce Tureens, Cheese Trays, Salad Bowls, Bakers,
etc.; 190 sets Chamber Services, Slop Jars, Water Jugs;
400 dozen of Tea and Breakfast cups and saucers in great
variety; 70 dozen of Tea plates; 100 dozen White bowls;
150 dozen of pints and mugs; 180 dozen of Jelly Cans,
Preserve Jars, Potting Pots; 80 dozen of Sauce Boats,
Mustards; 18 dozen of Dahlia Stands, Eye Baths; 18
dozen of Feeding Boats; 17 dozen of Mortars and Pestles,
and Paint Slabs, Jugs, Basins, &c.; and every article for
domestic purposes.

The BISCUIT WARE includes upwards of 700 dozen of
Table Ware, chiefly for printing, and 550 dozen of Tea and
Breakfast Ware for printing, and is particularly worthy of
the attention of the Trade.

Also will be sold the valuable FURNITURE . . . removed
from Swinton for the convenience of the sale—

Then follows an account of sideboard, piano, tables, carpets, etc.,
in short, the contents of a comfortably furnished middle-class household, presumably the personal possessions of Thomas Brameld himself.

The foregoing particulars are valuable since they indicate not only
the extent of Brameld production, but also the fact that concurrently
with the production of porcelain, earthenware too, continued to be
manufactured. For details of the sale see Appendix (p. 140) below.

CHAPTER IX

THE SCATTERED SHARDS

After that, the embers. The stock had gone. The plaster of Paris and earthenware moulds were dispersed, and sold variously. It is said that one mould of Conisbro' Castle went to Mexbro', and that of the fine lotus vase, passed into the hands of people at the Kilnhurst Pottery. The recipe for the renowned brown glaze became the property of the Baguleys. Thomas Brameld seems to have worked the flint mill from 1842 to 1844, but his day was done. He remained in Swinton, and for the rest of his days lived in comfort. (It is said that George Frederic lived with him). His fairly affluent condition remained, and still remains, something of a mystery. How was it possible, after suffering losses of such magnitude, to maintain the status of an independent gentleman? One can only conclude that he had private reserves. In any case the Earl would not press his late tenant too hard. So far as we know, John Wager continued to decorate wares in London.

Thomas Brameld did not live long to enjoy his retirement. He died on November 23rd, 1850; his brother John Wager in 1851; and George Frederic Brameld, on June 3rd, 1853.

John Brameld, the first proprietor, had been buried at Wath, but his sons, Thomas and George Frederic, lie side by side in the lee of the northward churchyard wall at Swinton. Beside Thomas rests his wife Jane, who died in 1854. A little removed from these three, is the headstone of Charles Wager Brameld, the only surviving son of John Wager, who was presumably buried in London.

Thomas left four sons, three became C. of E. clergymen; the fourth, a doctor (see *The Connoisseur*, June, 1967).

One intriguing tombstone in Swinton Churchyard is erected to a B. C. Wager of Ackworth "who departed this life at Swinton Pottery, 1st August, 1824, aged 57". The inscription implies that he was employed there, and accident apart, may have collapsed at work. Most probably he was a relative of the Mr. Wager who in 1829, had charge of the farm.

* * * *

After 1842 a small portion of the works was taken over by Isaac Baguley, the late manager of the gilding department, who carried on until his death in 1855. He was succeeded by his son, Alfred, who in 1865 moved to Mexborough. For a time Baguley retained the griffin mark, but as the Earl objected, the final form of the Baguley imprint became "The Rockingham Works, Mexbro". It is stated that Baguley was allowed to use the old crest only for wares commissioned for

Wentworth House, but even this provision must have lapsed. A brown glaze and gilt butter dish once in use on the Wentworth tables, now in possession of the authors, is marked simply, "Rockingham Works, Mexbro, Baguley".

The Baguley's decorated with excellent effect, unglazed wares purchased from other factories.

The curious may be interested to learn that after Thomas Brameld's relatively short working of the flint mill, some time later this came into the hands of James Parker, a former workman, by whom grinding was continued until 1887, the ground flint being sold to different potteries in the district.

I. and I. Walker then took over for twelve months. After that the mill closed down, and about 1910 the engine, boilers, and milling machinery were demolished and sold as scrap iron.

The recipe for the old Rockingham glaze as made by the Bramelds passed from Alfred Baguley to Mr. Bowman Heald of the Kilnhurst Pottery. He had been a friend of Baguley's for twenty years or more, and had done a great deal of work for him. It was from Mr. Heald who was alive in 1915, that Oxley Grabham, author of *Yorkshire Potteries, Pots and Potters*, contained in the Annual Report of the Yorkshire Philosophical Society for 1915, obtained most of this information.

*   *   *   *

Llewellyn Jewitt relates that when he visited the old pottery in the 1870's, the place was a "sad and desolate looking wilderness". The buildings had many of them been removed, and others were being demolished. "In the centre", he continued, "stands a building bearing the almost defaced words—*This Way to the China Room*". But almost all had gone; only pottery fragments scattered in and among the "shard rucks" remained.

Today, after varied fortunes, including service as a small-pox hospital, a storehouse, and an habitable cottage, the great Waterloo Kiln still stands, a gloomy monolith towering above the roofs of modern semi-detached houses. Grilles guard an interior now quite empty, and stout railings surround the whole. A grass-grown area runs towards the road. Here are some of the discard mounds, and digging not deeply, one is able to unearth fragments of pottery, pieces of willow pattern, jug handles and the like ...

We visited the pottery site, a day or two after the great gales of February, 1962. In the coppice across the road, large trees had been blown down, and among the exposed roots gleamed fragments of wares, both decorated and plain. One piece impressed "Brameld" we retained as a forlorn souvenir.

We retraced our steps and on the Wath side discovered the gateway, where a stone cottage—formerly the print house—still stands. A companion building on the other side, once the counting house, had been pulled down in recent years. From thence we turned to the Flint Mill pond. Of the shell of the mill, which survived into this century, there is no trace. The pond remains. Oral tradition has it that discontented workmen "getting back" on overlookers, or it may be concealing imperfect creations, tossed wares into the Flint Mill pond. Watching boys who fished from the banks, one wondered what the placid surface really concealed.

Other problems tease the mind. What became of the Bramelds' business papers? Did the kilns receive them? Where are George Frederic's Russian diaries? Where are his order books? There is a figure in Rotherham Museum of a Russian lady with baskets, decorated in blue and gold, identical with that produced by the St. Petersburg Imperial Pottery in the early part of the nineteenth century. Did George Frederic bring this back in his baggage, and did the Bramelds reproduce it?

There are Bramelds in the district who claim descent from the potters' line, but records are tenuous and lead to nowhere in particular. The only authentic family tree is contained in a little book, limited to fifty copies, the text of which drawn mainly from Jewitt, was published by a certain H. G. Brameld in 1910.

We have been unable to secure a portrait of any one of the Brameld family. Rotherham Clifton Park Museum has a large oil-painting depicting a review of Militia on Brinsworth Common in 1804. Recalling that both William and Thomas were commissioned in this force, we turned hopefully to the picture, but alas! while there was a bold equestrian study of Earl Fitzwilliam and other principal officers, the lower ranks showed blurred, anonymous faces. Curious it is that such talented men, accustomed to plying brush and paint, and having about them those equally gifted, have left nothing in terms of portraiture. But then the Bramelds were not socially important. They were in "trade". No member of the family sat upon the Bench.

The nearest approach we have made to a personal association with the Bramelds and their workmen, has been through a descendant of the Baguley family, who treasures certain relics of Rockingham in its heyday.

The collection includes a miniature of Isaac Baguley—a clean-shaven, self-assured man, replete in the plain black stock of the period; a mahogany box with brass fittings, inscribed "Peach Bowl", which was used to convey one piece of the Royal Service on its journey south, and subsequently returned empty; a pair of porcelain shirt studs, each decorated with a tiny fox's head; a broach miniature of a female Biblical character; Isaac's personal writing desk, complete with sandbox and other receptacles. Perhaps the most interesting item of the whole collection, is one of the original pattern books, resembling in size and appearance a medium-sized ledger, much thumbed and worn, but each page containing sketch studies for patterns, these annotated with pencillings dealing with one aspect or another of decoration. Since the book bears the name "Tommy Brameld", it is safe to infer that the senior partner was so addressed by his brethren and friends. It is possible that Isaac Baguley used certain patterns in the book, though from the nature of his output—glazing, gilding, etc.—reproduction could not have been to any great extent. We have been privileged to see two similar pattern books, owned by another of Isaac Baguley's descendants. As we have related, the Baguley family found it profitable to retain their connection with the Rockingham name and reputation. When Alfred Baguley, the son of Isaac, vacated the pottery, he issued a leaflet, a copy of which we have before us—

GLASS AND CHINA ROOMS, HIGH ST., MEXBRO'.
ALFRED BAGULEY most respectfully announces to the Nobility, Gentry, and the Public generally, that he has REMOVED FROM THE OLD ROCKINGHAM WORKS, SWINTON, to a new establishment situate at the above address ...
The Rooms are well-stocked with a great variety of ARTICLES IN CHINA, GLASS, and EARTHENWARE, which will he trusts well repay a visit previous to purchasing. The stock consists of Beautiful Dinner, Dessert, Breakfast, Tea, Coffee, and Toilet Services, Glass, etc.; especially the far-famed Rockingham China, which he continues to manufacture in its elegant and endless varieties.
Minton's and Copeland's China Matched to order.
Painting and Gilding Executed on the Premises.
Families may be waited upon with Patterns by addressing to A.B., Glass and China Rooms, Mexbro', near Rotherham.

Alfred Baguley's claim to continue manufacturing the "far-famed Rockingham China ... in its elegant and endless varieties" was, we fear, no more than an optimistic gesture. His means were too limited. Perhaps he hoped some day to take up where the Bramelds left off. Really, he worked in the afterglow of that royal reputation.

*　*　*　*

To sum up—what was the "Rockingham" contribution to the field of ceramic art? Here one feels, no deftly tagged label like "neo-rococo" for example, quite meets the mark. Subtle changes and permutations

PLATE IX

a. Creamware dessert side dish, painted in enamel colours.
$9\frac{1}{2} \times 7$in. (BRAMELD $+1$ *impressed*). *T. A. Lockett.*

b. (*Left*) Earthenware hot-water plate, transfer printed in blue
with the Willow pattern. Diam. $9\frac{3}{4}$in. (BRAMELD and a heart-
shaped device, *impressed*). *Mr. and Mrs. A. A. Eaglestone.*
(*Right*) Dessert side dish, transfer printed in pale blue with the
Willow pattern. 8in. $\times 7\frac{1}{2}$in. (BRAMELD *impressed*). *T. A.
Lockett.*

PLATE X

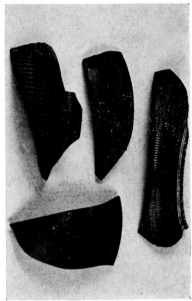

a. (*Above left*) Two black basalt fragments excavated on the factory site, from the lid and shoulder of the teapot in c. *Sheffield City Museum.*

b. (*Above right*) Black basalt fragments found on the Rockingham site.

c. Black basalt teapot with moulded floral emblems and a crest with the motto TRIA JUNCTA IN UNO. Length 10in. Ht. 6in. (Unmarked, see a.). *Private collection.*

of style, intermediate influences—"Empire" and "Regency"—had played a part.

They worked in a time of transition, imitating, adapting. "The almost indefinable water-shed", says Ralph Dutton, "between the prevalence of good taste and bad may be said to have synchronised approximately with the death of George IV". This being so, they were of the early dispensation.

But less aesthetical factors also prevailed. In the early years of the young Queen, certain innovations, particularly relating to household equipment, took place. The introduction of the sulphur match (one box for the kitchen, and one for the parlour) drove out the spill vase. Such as remained reverted to simple adornment. As literacy increased (the Penny Post ushered in a letter writing period) the ornate porcelain inkstand yielded to plainer shapes in glass. As medical knowledge extended, "Leech Jars" and the like became cumbrous anachronisms. The four poster bedstead was being replaced by smaller frames of cast-iron and brass. (Porcelain bedsteads never proved successful). Equipment for the table was decorated less elaborately. (The Baguley service in brown and gold for Wentworth House is a case in point). It became less the habit on birthdays and Christmas days to acquire the delicate and fragile porcelain knick-nacks which had once been so popular.

As sanitation extended and ventilation improved, the pastille burner (like the spill vase) reverted to adornment. Newer oil lamps, and the introduction of gas, eclipsed candelabra, though the candlestick in plainer form remained for lighting up to bedrooms.

When steam-printing brought a flow of illustrated journals and books, the tendency to adorn plaques, plates, dishes, and even cups and saucers with views, diminished. Parian ware, its smooth ivory-hued composition showing up well to a background of patterned wall-paper, or to a dark wood surface, competed with the coloured figurines and more fragile biscuit wares. The middle classes looked for good plain or lightly decorated china; and the shops many of which were started about this time, stocked wares to hand. As fashions in pets changed, even the dainty poodles lost favour, being replaced by the ox-eyed spaniel or the sleek greyhound.

Nor must interior arrangement, household *decor*, be forgotten. In 1811, Rochefoucauld, a French visitor, observed a tendency in England to bring furniture forward to the centre of the room rather than line it around the walls after the manner of the eighteenth century. As time passed, and the habit increased, ornaments tended to be set anywhere. The informal medley had arrived—"what-nots", fans and grasses, and the like. In short, "contemporary style".

All these elements played some part in the Brameld decline of fortune . . .

By 1840, the Romantic Movement, upon which the Bramelds drew for inspiration, and which to some extent they served, had expended its force. They had caught an ebbing tide.

In the absence of private letters and personal diaries, it is difficult to assess the level of their culture, the books they read, the artists and musicians whom they admired. To the outward eye they were conventional Whigs, and members of the Established Church. (When the new church was erected at Swinton, it was John Brameld, who at his own expense, preserved the entrance arch of the old chapel). Throughout this vexed period they kept clear of political broils, never indulged in law suits, were consistently faithful fathers and husbands. We have already mentioned that three of Thomas's sons became priests in the Church of England.

But they were artists too, accepting that affinity with Nature voiced by Rousseau and Wordsworth, though much nearer the latter than the former. It is not without significance that their most ambitious piece, the Wentworth Rhinoceros Vase, should be decorated with scenes from *Don Quixote*, the work which lured young Wordsworth to his dream—

> Once in the stillness of a summer's noon
> While I was seated in a rocky cave
> By the sea-side, perusing, as it chanced
> The famous history of the errant knight
> Recorded by Cervantes, these same thoughts
> Beset me, and to a height unusual rose
> While listlessly I sate, and having closed
> The book, had turned my eyes toward the wide sea
> On poetry and geometric truth . . .

It may have been an unconscious gesture which inspired the decoration; but of all the "Rockingham" wares this is the only one directly related to romantic fiction, or indeed to Literature of any kind. Was the knight of de la Mancha after all, their symbol? "Too sanguine", Mr. Bowns, the agent, had said of them, but as between potter and patron who was the Quixote and who Sancho Panza? "It is easy", remarks Lytton Strachey, "to talk of defeat and failure, but . . . if one considers those records of achievement and of thought, one begins to wonder whether such things can be measured by such terms. One seems to discern in them something less unfortunate than failure, and something, perchance, more splendid than success".

These words may well apply to the Brameld story. They fail in business at a grim time when manufacturers (who were not artists) failed also. But the inspired foray, the bright panache of that porcelain period, merits an honourable place in ceramic annals.

PART TWO

THE WARES

---

1. INTRODUCTION.

This account of the production of the pottery from 1745 to 1842, has been separated from the formal history in order that each may be read in its entirety without any break in the narrative. It should be remembered when reading the ensuing pages that the output of the works, the designs produced, the styles, and many other artistic factors, were conditioned by economic considerations, and by the changing pattern of ownership. The formal history should be constantly borne in mind when reading of the wares produced.

There seems in certain quarters, to be confusion as to what is, and what is not, "Rockingham"; so many wrong attributions are made, and so few writers and "experts" seem to have a sound knowledge of the actual wares, that we have felt it necessary to document and authenticate individual pieces rather more precisely than is the normal custom. We have examined a good many collections both public and private, but for descriptive purposes we have largely confined our attention to eight principal collections, four public, and four private. The public collections are in the Victoria and Albert, the Sheffield, York St. Mary's and the Rotherham museums.

The collection at the V. & A. is rather small, and not really comprehensive, though it contains some outstanding individual items. The Sheffield collection is larger, well-presented and clearly labelled. The York (Yorkshire) Museum has an even greater number of pieces, with one large case of porcelain very well displayed. The pottery and earthenware is scattered in a number of cases. The Rotherham Museum has undoubtedly the finest collection, and is the best displayed. Even so, shortage of space has meant that some of the plainer, though not necessarily less interesting wares, have had to be stored in cupboards under the display cabinets. (York too has many pieces not on public display).

Throughout the text we have indicated, wherever necessary, in which of these collections notable pieces can be found, so that any interested in further detailed knowledge will know where fully authenticated items can be seen. (Other museums, for example Doncaster and Nottingham have "Rockingham" amongst their collections, but to these we have not made direct textual reference).

A few references are made to our own small joint collection, but the three main private collections to which we have had access, are those of Mr. W. Mason of Rotherham, Mr. M. Redfern of Dorking, and Mrs. B. M. L. Llewellyn of Abergavenny. All three collectors have been most kind, and have given generously of their time and experience to assist us. All three have outstanding collections, and in the case of Mrs. Llewellyn, far larger than anything to be seen on public display. We have referred in the text to marked or clearly authenticated pieces in these collections. Where there has been doubt concerning the authenticity of a piece, or where we have had to take the word of others, we have used the phrase "attributed to Rockingham" unless we ourselves have seen and confirmed the genuineness of the ware.

A final point concerns the use of the word "porcelain". "Rockingham" is not a true soft paste porcelain because of its relatively high bone-ash content; nor is it identical with the "bone china" of the later nineteenth century. Throughout therefore, we used the three terms "porcelain", "bone china" or simply "china", as synonymous. All of them refer to the translucent wares, as distinct from the opaque pottery and earthenware.

N.B. (1973). It should be recorded that the W. Mason collection was dispersed upon the owner's death some years ago. Mrs Llewellyn's fine collection was sold in three parts at Sotheby's during 1972-73. Of the four Museum collections noted, the Sheffield collection has significantly increased since 1964; the Rotherham Museum has had a great many additions, and is now quite outstanding.

2. POTTERY AND EARTHENWARE 1745-1806.

During the twenty years when Butler was proprietor of the Pottery, production seems to have been confined entirely to common manufactured goods—pots, cups, basins, ewers and the like made of earthenware, and bricks and tiles from the "common yellow clay". These simple domestic items would be sold in the surrounding villages as well as to Wentworth, but being objects of everyday use, would not be treasured. It would seem likely that Butler did not mark his wares in any way; had he done so nineteenth century collectors would have recorded the fact and retained specimens. The chance of any of Butler's work being found now, and definitely identified, is exceedingly remote.

Much the same can be said of the thirteen years when William Malpass was the principal proprietor. Obviously, he too did not mark his wares in any way, or if he did, no examples have been recorded. We can only presume that Malpass continued to make the same types of pottery as Butler.

The entry of Thomas Bingley into the firm in 1778 seems to have provided a stimulus; from this date expansion took place, both in the volume of production and the variety of wares produced. Once again, one is hesitant to make a categorical statement about the kind of pottery made. Pieces marked BINGLEY (impressed into the ware) have been recorded, and from these it has been assumed that yellow as well as brownware was made; possibly blue and white earthenware dinner, tea and coffee services were produced. We have been unable to locate any of these marked pieces, and any unmarked ones which have survived, would be quite indistinguishable from similar wares made at many Staffordshire potteries. The brownware made at this period, crude and utilitarian, may well be reposing in museum cabinets labelled "Nottingham Ware" or simply "Staffordshire". Blackware may have been made before 1785, but this too, is quite impossible to differentiate from the work of other potteries.

Clearly the connection with the Leeds Pottery was a turning point in the history of the works, and made a technical difference much more than the infusion of Bingley's capital had done. At forty-four, John Brameld too, would be a man of mature experience, and resembling the character of his descendants, anxious to expand and to try new forms; but for the time being it is the Leeds influence which predominates. For the next twenty-one years—the full term of the shareholders lease—production at Swinton was geared to the requirements of the Leeds Pottery as a whole. The Leeds price list was used, and the Leeds pattern book adopted over a wide range. One of the price lists recorded is headed, "Greens, Bingley & Co., Swinton Pottery", and is an exact replica of the Leeds list. A later catalogue dated, "Swinton

See Llewellyn Jewitt and the catalogue of the Boynton Collection.

Pottery, 1st February, 1796" is headed, "Greens, Hartley & Co., Swinton Pottery, make, sell, and export wholesale all sorts of Earthenware, Cream, Coloured or Queens, Nankeen Blue, Tortoise Shell, Fine Egyptian Black, Brown China, etc., etc. All the above shapes enamelled, printed, or ornamented with gold and silver". This announcement though similar to the Leeds lists of the period, is not an exact copy as was the earlier one.

A much fuller list of the Pottery's output in the 1790's, also on record, is worth quoting at length in order to illustrate the great expansion that had taken place since the advent of the "Leeds Gentlemen". In creamware alone, services were obtainable in seven main shapes: "Paris, Bath, concave, royal, queen's, feather and shell-edge". All these were "Printed or enamelled with coats-of-arms, crests, cyphers, lanscapes, &c.; also blue printed Nankeen patterns". Then follows a list of separate items available in cream—"Dishes, covers, compotiers, tureens, plates, butter-tubs, baking dishes, nappies, glass-trays, fruit plates, fruit baskets pierced and plain, ice-cellars, candlesticks, inkstands, bidets, &c., furnished castors, tureen ladles, chocolate stands, quintal flower horns, radish dishes, crosses with holy-water cup, ice-pails, broad mugs, bowls, ewers, basins, &c.; milk ewers, tea and coffee pots, tea canisters, chocolate cups and saucers, &c., &c."

In addition to this extensive range of creamware, there were presumably various patterns and designs for products in plain earthenware, blue transfer printed, tortoiseshell, and black and brown ware. In Sheffield Museum a blackware jug bearing the date 1802 and the words, "BEER, Richard Sammons", is ascribed to Swinton. From what must have been a considerable output over a twenty-years' period, only a handful of specimens have been ascribed to the factory; some of these are marked BINGLEY, and therefore could relate to the earlier period. It is obvious that a great deal of the surviving output of Swinton—for lack of conclusive evidence of its true origin—has been assigned to another factory, namely Leeds. This must be especially so of the creamware.

Except for the impressed BINGLEY already mentioned, there are no recorded marks for this period which can be authenticated. It is probable that the wares were not marked in any way, though it is just possible that the marks of the Leeds Pottery were used without discrimination on goods made at Swinton. A number of pieces bearing their owner's name have been attributed to the Swinton works. One such is a two-handled cup inscribed "William Brameld" and the date, 1788 (William would then be sixteen). It is just possible that he made his own piece. Parts of the cup are decorated with transfer printing in blue, said to resemble the famous "willow pattern". Whether this can really be taken as evidence that "willow pattern" was produced at Swinton as early as 1788, is somewhat doubtful, but it is not impossible, for this entirely English design was introduced at the Caughley factory about 1780, Thomas Minton being credited with the invention.

It has often been asserted that the one article of manufacture peculiar to the Swinton Pottery at this period was the ware known as "Brown China", subsequently as "Rockingham Ware". This is, of course, not a true china, but a white or cream-coloured earthenware dipped in glaze heavily stained with manganese oxide. The glaze, and the resultant shade of reddish brown which remains on the pot after firing, is thought to be a special characteristic of the factory, lasting from its introduction about 1785 until the closing of the works in 1842. Pieces dipped in this glaze are not uniform in colour, but since the glaze ran down the body during firing, are lighter at the top. The shading from top to bottom, from light to dark with no uniformity, is most effective.

We believe that there are several different types of brown-glaze pottery, all of which are usually designated, "Brown china" or "Rockingham Ware". Clearly many of these have no connection with the Swinton factory. It is in the type of glaze used, that the real difference is discernable. Firstly, there is a common brown glaze which varies from a golden syrupy colour to a dark treacle hue. This variation depends upon the consistency of the glaze and the number of times the piece has been dipped. Many Staffordshire potteries have used this type of brown glaze for all kinds of wares for many years. It was used at Swinton from a quite early date—possibly during the tenancy of Bingley—and certainly from 1785 onwards.

A second type of glaze, possibly introduced at Swinton in the 1780's, is a modification of the earlier formula which produces a fuller, richer brown, a more mottled and controlled streakiness, and a finer surface less prone to "crackle". This type of glaze can be seen on wares from other potteries as well as on those emanating from Swinton.

The third type of glaze which is characteristic of the wares made by the Bramelds, is of a much higher standard. It is basically a chocolate brown, but frequently one of the effects of the manganese oxide is to produce a purplish iridescence or bloom on the piece when held against the light. We believe that this glaze was the invention of the Bramelds, and that the only comparable glaze was that used by the Baguleys, who are said to have inherited the secret from their former masters. It was with this third type of glaze that the majority of the brownware pieces, and the tea, chocolate and coffee pots, were finished during the Brameld period. This would account for the fact that the product of the Don Pottery—which clearly succeeded Swinton as the Leeds subsidiary—was markedly inferior to the brown china made by the Bramelds after 1806. Had the formula for the glaze been Leeds property it would certainly have gone with them, and have been used subsequently in their factories. Brown china was a popular line. Thus we conjecture that the Bramelds experimented with, and eventually introduced, an

86

improved glaze. The inferior glazes made up to 1806 are indistinguishable, except by detailed analysis, from the work of other factories making the ware. However, there is clearly scope for further inquiry into the exact nature of the glazes.

The two patterns in brown china which are best known, and of which examples are not hard to find, are the "snuff-taking squire", and the "Cadogan" tea or coffee pot.

The squire was a well-known figure from the late eighteenth and early nineteenth century potteries. Models for use as jugs, tea and coffee pots were made at a number of factories. At Swinton the squire may well have been modelled in earthenware with ordinary brown glaze as early as 1785. Later specimens moulded as teapots in the brown china, display the characteristic rich hue and firm glaze of what (after 1826) became known as "Rockingham ware." A few marked pieces have been recorded. The Cadogan pots, which were almost certainly not made before 1806, will be considered in a later chapter.

*   *   *   *

The collector, or would be collector, of pottery from Swinton for the whole of this period, 1745-1806, is faced with a difficult task. As we have indicated the Butler and Malpass periods are virtually uncollectable. The Bingley period offers no better prospect. The fact that a few pieces marked BINGLEY have been recorded offers dubious hope, for the mark could refer to the Greens, Bingley period also. In none of the collections we have seen have we been able to find a clearly authenticated Bingley piece.

The pottery of the later years of the Leeds ownership would seem to be more abundant. However, as so little is known about possible marks, a detailed knowledge of the output of Leeds, and other potteries manufacturing similar goods (including Wedgwood), would be the likeliest approach to sorting out what really belongs to Swinton. A further complicating factor is that many of the wares made during this period were in form continued by the Bramelds right through to 1842, and if not marked by them would be difficult to place.

Clearly there is scope for enthusiastic collectors who would be prepared to work hard, and take a few risks. One encouraging aspect is that prices for pieces belonging to this time, should be relatively low. Small pieces could well be obtained in the right places for shillings rather than pounds.

3. POTTERY AND EARTHENWARE, 1806-1842.
(i) Brownware.

On assuming complete control of the Pottery the Bramelds were anxious to strengthen their position and recapture the markets enjoyed before the break with the "Leeds Gentlemen". Moreover, strong competition could be expected from the Don Pottery, which taking advantage of the immensely popular election in 1807 of Lord Milton for the County, produced in that year their celebrated "Jumper Jugs" portraying a brashly humorous character who was employed to amuse and enliven Whig supporters. (This piece, by the way, is often wrongly ascribed to the Brameld works). The "Jumper Jug" had a large sale throughout Yorkshire.

No great change in the production of the Swinton Factory seems to have taken place in the early days after the change of ownership. A price list for this period is exactly the same as that issued before 1806, except that the heading "Greens, Bingley" has been crossed out, and a new heading, "Brameld & Co." substituted. It was however, about this time that the celebrated "Cadogan" teapots were first made. (Plate IIa).

These pots are curious pieces. The body is tall, but narrow; the whole pot somewhat elongated in appearance. There is no lid to the piece; the top being decorated with foliage in relief. This decoration has been described as resembling coffee beans and flowers, though others have seen it as peaches and peach blossom. Both the spout and the handle have a thin branch of foliage joined to them from the main body of the pot. In the centre of the base is a hole through which the pot is filled. The principle of construction is that of an unspillable inkwell. A tube runs from the hole in the base to within half an inch of the top of the pot; thus when it has been filled from the base, the pot can safely be righted without the liquid being spilled. Neither tea nor coffee can be brewed in it. The operation has to be performed separately in another pot. The principal use may well have been as hot-water vessels.

There has been considerable confusion in the past as to when this oddity first appeared. We feel sure that it was not until after 1806. Several points confirm this view. Had the pots been produced before this date, the design would surely have been taken by the Leeds people when they left. It is true that had they wished to copy the "Cadogans" they could have done so at any time—as indeed the Spode-Copeland factory did[1]—but it would have been easier for Leeds to have claimed immediate right.

[1] The Spode factory used the "Cadogan" design for teapots in the early 19th century, and they were all marked "Spode" or "Copeland". Minton's too, produced "Cadogan" teapots, but not until 1877, and all their pieces too were marked.

It is generally agreed that "Cadogans" achieved their popularity after 1810. This was, of course, an era of slow communications, but if such novelties—for this they were—had been made as far back as the 1790's, they would have "caught on" before 1810. A final, and most important point, concerns the marking of the pots. Jewitt stated that the mark "Rockingham" impressed in script (not printed) on the bottom of one of the pots was "the earliest used by these works". Because of this assertion it has been assumed that this "earliest" of the marks, was used before the Brameld period. Jewitt's proposition seems highly questionable to us; yet it has been accepted without hesitation by most writers on the subject. We cannot believe that ordinary potters, tenants of one of the most influential oligarchs in England, would presume to use as a trademark the name of their former noble landowner. What really seems to have happened is that *after 1826*, the owner being the Earl, and the factory officially styled "The Rockingham Works", the name "Rockingham Ware" became attached to the characteristic "brown china" produced at the factory. Thus it became habitual to give the name "Rockingham Ware" not only to goods produced at Swinton after 1826, but also to similar wares produced before this date—incidentally to similar wares from other factories. Jewitt, writing at least twenty years after the Bramelds had ceased to manufacture, made a wrong deduction. In a word, the pieces marked in the way Jewitt describes are *after* 1826, the mark quoted being one of the many varients used from that date onwards. It should be noted that the teapots were known as "Cadogan" rather than "Rockingham" pots.

The origin of the pots, of how they came to acquire the name "Cadogan", is not at all clear. Accounts which exist seem to have been addled with the passage of time. John Guest, *Historic Notices of Rotherham*, 1879, states that the Marquis and Marchioness of Rockingham brought a coffee pot and a tea pot from Dresden, and that these were kept in a glass case at Wentworth for many years. Subsequently, Earl Fitzwilliam took out the coffee pot, and asked Thomas Brameld if he could produce anything like it.[1] Brameld referred the problem to his chemist, William Speight, who made three specimens, one of which was selected for manufacture. Jewitt on the other hand, says the pots were modelled on an example of green Indian ware, alleged to have been brought from abroad by the Rockinghams or the Hon. Mrs. Cadogan, and preserved fifty or sixty years before it was copied. A local commentator maintained that during the eighteenth century,

[1] It is interesting to note that Guest says the pot was given to Thomas Brameld. If such was the case it is further evidence that "Cadogans" were not made before 1806. Thomas was only nineteen in that year, and thus could hardly have been more than a year out of his apprenticeship; in fact this might suggest that "Cadogans" were not made until after 1813 when Thomas was the senior partner of the three brothers.

Mrs. Cadogan visited China, and brought back with her a curious teapot or rice-spirit vessel, which reposed at Wentworth for some forty years, and being seen by the owners of the Rockingham Works, was manufactured by them in the famous brownware. It has been alleged that the name was acquired because the first one was made for Mrs. Cadogan.

From such conflicting evidence one concludes that the "Cadogans" were free adaptations of peach-shaped Chinese wine pots. Such a pot was in the possession of Earl Fitzwilliam. In 1806, or shortly thereafter, Thomas Brameld successfully produced a copy of this oriental oddity In some way, the Hon. Mrs. Cadogan, or originally the Earl of Cadogan, was connected with these vessels, which henceforth bore the family name.

"Cadogans" were made in a variety of sizes, and in several different colours. The normal-sized pot stands about seven inches in height, whereas the miniature, or "baby Cadogans" are only three and a half inches high. Specimens larger than seven inches exist, though these are more rarely seen. The majority were finished in the brown manganese oxide glaze typical of the Rockingham ware—and are said to have been dipped in the glaze and fired three times. Quite a proportion of the pots have the foliage decoration picked out in gold, and this applies to both ordinary and miniature. "Cadogans" with a different coloured glaze are very rare, but they were apparently made in white, in a deep, clear blue, in green, in a patterned green and blue, and "with a peach-like bloom on a deep mushroom glaze". There are other variations of colour.

Many of the pots are unmarked. Those which are marked usually bear one or the other of the "Brameld" imprints (see pp. 132-134). However, several other marks were used. "Rockingham" impressed in flowing script we have already noticed. "ROCKINGHAM" impressed in capital letters in several sizes of stamp would date from the same period (after 1826). CADOGAN, impressed in capital letters is also recorded. Other interesting impressed marks are, NORFOLK, MORTLOCK, MORTLOCKS, MORTLOCK'S CADOGAN, and MORTLOCK'S ROYAL ROCKINGHAM. The last four are indicative of the firm's connection with the Oxford Street pottery and china merchants. The first mark would be imprinted for the convenience of the factory to identify goods intended for their markets in Norfolk. The other four were sold by Mortlock's. It has been stated that the Prince Regent bought one or more "Cadogans" from Mortlock's, and as this became known there was a resultant rush of orders for the pots. Orders for one year ran to the value of £900.

* * * *

In addition to the "Cadogans", a variety of products were made in brownware. This class of goods was of sound quality and tended to be quite light in weight. It is not particularly easy to find examples of the "Brown China" which can be definitely ascribed to the Bramelds

(Plate Ia). They are said to have produced tea and coffee services, jugs, drinking cups and mugs, but many of the examples we have seen, have on close examination turned out to be the work of Isaac or Alfred Baguley.[1] The Don Pottery too was making brown china in competition with the Swinton Works.

Certain more unusual items can be more confidently ascribed to the Bramelds. They made shoe warmers. These were hollow vessels in the shape of a shoe which were to be filled with hot water and placed in ladies shoes before use—one would imagine a tricky business! In Weston Park Museum, Sheffield, there is an interesting brown ware piece also in the form of a shoe. This, with three holes in the top, was probably used as an inkwell, or as a pen stand. Certain large jugs have been identified. These are most elegantly shaped, and have gold ornamentation on the stopper and down the body of the jug, the neck of which is octagonal. Hot water jugs, and ordinary tea, chocolate and coffee pots in a number of designs and bearing a variety of marks, are also authentic Brameld productions. Examples of these can be seen in the main public collections (Plate IIa).

Earthenware furniture-supports, or elevators, moulded in the face of a man or woman, or as a lion's head, have been attributed to Swinton; and the manufacture of these would probably continue under the Bramelds, though we have no record of any one so marked. Stirrup cups in the shape of a dog's or fox's head in brownware, were made at a number of potteries during the early nineteenth century. Some specimens have been attributed to the Bramelds, but again, we have no record of a marked piece.

It is quite possible that the Bramelds made "frog mugs", moustache cups, muffin dishes, candlesticks and candleholders in the brown china. The scarcity of marked pieces is a serious drawback. We have mentioned that Isaac and Alfred Baguley used the Brameld brown china glaze. It is known that both Baguley's had complete access to the Brameld pattern books, from which they took designs for the decoration of the wares they bought, and that many of their products were unmarked. However, much of the Baguley decoration is done on real, i.e., bone-china rather than on earthenware, whereas the Bramelds very rarely used the brown glaze on their porcelain goods. This is of some help in attribution.

It must be emphasised that, "Cadogans" apart, many of the brown china patterns were in use before 1806, and the Bramelds probably continued to produce these without particular alteration until the pottery closed in 1842. The dating therefore, of unmarked pieces is a tentative

In 1865, Baguley's son Alfred, moved to Mexbro', and there continued to decorate china and pottery bought in the "white" from Minton; Brown,-Westhead, Moore & Co.; Powell, Bishop and Stonier. A. Baguley died in 1891. Old Mexbro' inhabitants recall the kilns.

matter, and much depends upon close inspection of the shape of the ware, and upon glazing in particular. Apart from the NORFOLK, CADO-GAN and MORTLOCK marks on the "Cadogans", no special marks have been found on this brownware. Pieces which are marked at all, carry the normal variants of the "Brameld" and "Rockingham" marks.

(ii) Creamware and Stoneware

Although brownware, and "Cadogan" pots in particular, are the best known items of Brameld pottery in the period 1806 to 1842, cream-ware must have been the mainstay of the factory's production in the first twenty years of this period. A large proportion would be exported, or produced to order for the Eastern Counties and the Scottish trade. The remainder would be sold locally.

Patterns were much the same as in the "Leeds Period", but certain improvements and modifications were made in order to attract fresh custom. A popular design introduced at this time was the Don Quixote pattern, the work of T. Stothard, a prolific artist of the day. Pieces of various kinds were decorated with this design, and complete dinner services were made with a variety of transfer printed scenes from the Cervantes classic. The knight's adventures (for reasons stated elsewhere) had a ready appeal (Plate Ib).

Popular taste inclined to pastoral scenes, flower studies, ruined castles and abbeys. The potters responded so that the transfer printed ware of the period is typically "Romantic" in design. Two detailed examples will serve. In both Rotherham and Sheffield museums there are plates and dishes from a dinner service bearing a blue underglaze transfer picture of a sturdy woodman returning home to his humble cottage among the trees. His child meets him at the gate, and his wife sits beside the door at her spinning wheel (Plate Ib). A second example can be found in the Sheffield Museum, and Mrs. Eaglestone has a pair of dishes with a similar design in her collection. The picture is an underglaze transfer in deep blue, depicting a young man with a fishing rod conversing with a young maid. Trees, a bridge, a ruin, a lake, and distant mountains form the background, while a floral pattern decorates the rim (Plate IIb). The pattern is entitled, *Castle of Rochefort*.

The willow pattern was also much used; a marked example can be seen in Sheffield Museum. In the Rotherham Museum, several simple floral designs can be seen on creamware and pearlware plates.

One of the most interesting and unusual designs is a pattern with a twisted tree, the large flowers, butterflies and curiously poised birds, printed in both blue and green as an underglaze transfer (Plate IIb). On some pieces, overglaze colours were applied to various parts of this design, and gilding too has been noted. Mrs. Thompson, of Rawmarsh, has a wonderfully preserved dinner service in this pattern, printed in green with gilt ornamentation; a family heirloom. This most attractive pattern was possibly intended to compete with the popular "Indian Tree" design. Llandeg's blackberry pattern also decorates creamware services. The blackberry motif covers only the rim of the plate; in the centre is a printed flower. In Mrs. Llewellyn's collection are to be found two interesting pieces; one depicts horses and hounds at the height of the chase;[1] the second is a homely equine study of a rocking horse, underneath which is printed, "For Sarah".

These are a few of the patterns and designs to be found in Brameld cream earthenware. It is impossible in a work of this limited scope to give details of all the known variants. One must stress however, that while the bulk of the creamware was made during the years 1806 to 1826, the production of earthenware continued until 1842. New designs new patterns and materials were being introduced until the last days of the pottery.

*   *   *   *

A fine cane-coloured stoneware was introduced probably before 1820 (Plate IIa). Jugs and mugs of this body are all that appear to have survived, and it is possible that these were the only items fashioned in this material. They are quite handsome; the cane colour is attractive and provides a good background for the applied relief decoration which encircles the piece. The decoration depicts cupids with musical instruments. The relief is usually in white or blue, though in Mrs. Llewellyn's collection of these pieces, green and chocolate coloured relief can also be seen. Another feature of the mugs is to be found in the handle. Where it meets the tip of the piece it is fashioned as the tail of a horse, half way down it changes into the leg, and ends in the hoof at the point where the handle rejoins the body of the jug. Examples are on view at the Victoria and Albert, Rotherham and York museums. All that we have examined are marked with an oval medallion or cartouche in the colour of the applied decoration. This bears a wreath of roses, thistles and shamrock round the border, and in the centre the name BRAMELD. The standard of these mugs and jugs is every bit as high as that of similar Wedgwood products. A certain amount of opaque stone china was also made, probably in the years 1810-26. Just how much was produced is difficult to assess, for very few examples survive. It may have been exported in considerable quantity, but we cannot be certain. Both Rotherham and Sheffield museums have examples of plates which indicate that the patterns used were simple floral transfers, and scenes as on the printed creamware. The marks on the stone china are interesting and quite elaborate. Details can be found on p.132.

The Bramelds green-glazed ware is really handsome. There are two distinctive features about it. First, the body of the ware is surprisingly light; second ,the glaze is lighter in colour and of a thinner consistency

[1] Illustrated in the Connoisseur Year Book, 1962.

than that used by Wedgwood and most of the other factories making similar pottery. The glaze too (on most pieces) has a remarkable iridescence when held against the light, the surface reflecting just those colours which are seen when petrol is lying on water. It is said that whole services, vases and other ornamental items were produced in the greenware, but only single plates are to be seen today, though some unmarked pieces may have been recorded as the work of Wedgwood or another factory. The plates are moulded with a number of different designs; the delicately veined cabbage-leaf pattern one of the most common. Several varients of embossed work are known. Some have leaves moulded around the rim of the plate; others have a mixture of leaves, and panels containing more criss-cross cane work. Certain plates have concentric circular incisions on the under side of the rim—a very distinctive feature. Green-glazed plates are rare. There are two in the Victoria and Albert Collection, and two in Rotherham Museum. We have also seen a few in private collections, notably in Mrs. Llewellyn's. So comparatively fragile are the plates, that all but a handful must have been broken (Plate Ia).

More fragile even, was the ware aptly described by Jewitt as "chalkbody". The manufacture of this extremely light earthenware was apparently discontinued because of the high percentage of loss during firing. Not only are pieces light, but they are also of a very clear white. None of the public galleries we have visited has a specimen of this ware, though there must be a number of pieces in private hands. The only examples within our notice are a pair of jugs in our own collection. These came to us from a life-long student of Rockingham, who had recognised them for what they were by the transfer "tree" pattern which was used extensively by the Bramelds on earthenware. They are, however, unmarked.

Shortly after they became proprietors of the Swinton Pottery, the Bramelds began to manufacture a type of creamware which enjoyed a considerable vogue for a few years. The earthenware itself was of a good sound quality, and again, quite light. The decoration of the pieces which were for dessert services was of the highest standard; each plate painted with a life size and quite realistic flower or plant study. The names of the plants so depicted were marked on the back of the plate or dish, usually in Latin. Thus, a fine painting of yellow blossom on one plate in the Victoria and Albert is marked "Dillwynia floribunda". In the same cabinet an unmarked, but similar study, of a carnation, ascribed to Swinton, has the name in English. These particular flower studies are attributed to the artist Collinson. It seems a great pity that so few examples of his work have survived, for he had a most accomplished touch. It must be added that the adjacent Don Pottery, and a number of other well-known factories were at this period making services similarly decorated. (The name of William Pegg at the Derby

PLATE XI

a.   Pierced dessert basket and stand, printed and enamelled with the "Twisted tree" pattern. Basket 8½in. × 5¾in. Stand 8¼in. × 6½in. (From a marked service). *Mr. and Mrs. A. A. Eaglestone.*

b.   Earthenware dessert basket, transfer printed in medium blue with the "Sweet peas" pattern. 9in. × 6in. Ht. 3in. (BRAMELD +4 *impressed*). *T. A. Lockett.*

PLATE XII

a. (*Above left*) Small earthenware stand, transfer printed in medium blue with the "Apple gatherers" pattern. Diam. 5¾in. (BRAMELD +6 *impressed*). *A. H. Dodson, Esq.*

b. (*Above right*) Earthenware plate with outline transfer printed Imari-type pattern and overglaze colours. Diam. 6in. (BRAMELD *impressed*). *Private collection.*

c. (*Below left*) Earthenware salad bowl underglaze printed and overglaze enamelled with the "Three urns" pattern. Diam. 9¾in. Ht. 4in. (Unmarked, see text). *T. A. Lockett.*

d. (*Below right*) Earthenware "Mess" plate with deep underglaze blue border, gilding and various legends (see text). Diam. 9in. (BRAMELD & BECKITT, PICCADILLY [*sic*] LONDON printed overglaze). *Mr. and Mrs. A. A. Eaglestone.*

factory is well-known in this connection). As the standard of their workmanship was also high, correct identification of unmarked pieces is no easy task.

Undoubtedly many other items were produced during these years. One such, a brightly decorated tub, about 2-ft. 6-in. high, used for many years at Wentworth in the Orangery, is now in Mr. W. Mason's collection. But few, if any other earthenware pieces have survived, or been correctly ascribed. The "lotus" vase which Jewitt selects as "one of the specialities of the Swinton Pottery" has not found its way into any public collection which we have covered. The vase, formed of upright leaves, and decorated with raised butterflies, was either enamelled or green glazed. It was without doubt a finely shaped piece of pottery— "a flower vase of surpassing beauty", commented Jewitt. Of other decorative pieces, little or nothing is known.

A list of marks on Brameld earthenware and pottery can be found on pp.132-4.

*   *   *   *

As we have indicated, Brameld pottery and earthenware is not particularly plentiful. Brownware pieces can be found frequently, but identification is a difficult business. The price of such items as "Cadogan" teapots is steadily rising—£7 to £12 is by no means excessive. Cane-coloured, green and chalk-body wares, are exceedingly scarce, but because so few dealers recognise them for what they really are, prices may not bear strict relation to rarity.

Transfer-printed cream, and ordinary earthenware, should not be highly priced. If £10 can buy a good porcelain plate, half of this should be more than sufficient to secure an earthenware plate or dish. Most of our own pieces have cost less than this.

When a pottery like Swinton, produced both earthenware and porcelain, collectors almost invariably concentrate their attention on the more attractive, decorative china pieces. The ordinary earthenware is not highly regarded, certainly in the past was less well-cared for, and being in constant use, much of it broken or severely damaged. This must have been the fate of special service crockery they manufactured for use in vessels like the *Forfarshire* of the Dundee and Hull Steam Packet Company. A specimen from the Dundee Museum was illustrated in *The Connoisseur*, July 1966, p. 172.

Having said so much, it may not be too late for some enthusiast to form a really comprehensive collection. It would certainly be a cheaper proposition than beginning with porcelain, though collecting would entail a good deal more patience, searching and serious study.

4. PORCELAIN 1826-42.

(a) Experimental: the artistic climate.

The success of the Pottery from 1810 to 1820 encouraged Thomas Brameld to experiment in the production of porcelain. 1820 is usually recorded as the year in which the experiments began, but there is no evidence to suggest that anything other than trial pieces were produced before 1825.

Jewitt mentions two trial pieces which he dated as 1820-22—unfortunately we have been unable to trace these. The oft-repeated assertion that the cost of porcelain experiments and production brought the firm to its knees in 1826 will not bear close scrutiny. Such experiments and the consequent cost of materials, may have imposed an additional burden, but the evidence we have found clearly indicates that the financial difficulties were the result of the general economic situation, and in particular of the large sums of money owed to the Bramelds by their overseas buyers.

When the Bramelds invited help from Earl Fitzwilliam in 1826, they intended to *begin* the full scale production of porcelain. They were not asking for funds to defray losses already incurred in its manufacture. We stress this point, because in what should have been the most reputable circles of ceramic dealing, we have frequently seen pieces labelled "Rockingham China, *circa* 1820". Sometimes one turns over such a piece to find the griffin and "Manufacturer to the King"—a mark not used before *1830*.

The earliest known authenticated piece of Rockingham porcelain is in Rotherham Museum. It is a cup. In script on the base is written "Rockingham China Works—Swinton 1826". We believe that this particular cup was finished and marked *before* the familiar stamp was prepared (Plate IVa). We cannot conceive that had the Bramelds been successfully manufacturing porcelain from 1820 they would have refrained for six years from marking any of their pieces. There is only one recorded instance of Rockingham porcelain bearing a mark which *could* date before 1826. This was noted by Thomas Boynton, and is listed in the catalogue of his collection. The mark is simply "Brameld" pencilled in red, and in script. Had any quantity of porcelain been made before 1826, more than one isolated example would have come to light. In fact, many pieces marked "*circa* 1820", would be more accurately described as "*circa* 1840". The latter months of 1825 are the very earliest that can be given for serious porcelain manufacture; even this may be too early. Production on a factory level for public sale would not begin until the late Spring of 1826.

* * * *

The porcelain made by the Bramelds during this period was of a very high quality. It consisted of bone ash (calcined animal bones),

Cornish stone, and china clay from St. Austell. The resultant paste is clean, fine, hard and clearly translucent. The glaze, though tending to craze in a very fine network on many pieces, gives the wares a soft, velvety, almost warm feel. It is pleasant to touch. The crazing is often so fine that very close inspection is needed to recognise it. There are many variations both in the composition of the paste and the quality of the glaze, but the overall standard is high. However thin the actual body of the piece, Rockingham china feels substantial—it has weight and solidity. Close scrutiny of a piece of Rockingham reveals the surface under the glaze to have the appearance of what one commentator has indicated as "crushed snow"; another has likened the texture to that of orange peel. These are rough and ready descriptions, but they provide one clue to the correct identification of a piece of Rockingham porcelain.

For sixteen years the Bramelds poured out a flood of articles made from these ingredients, and Rockingham porcelain acquired the somewhat invidious distinction of becoming a "status symbol". This was deceptive, for as the fashion changed so did the fortunes of the Bramelds. The prevalent style was "Revived Rococo", not directly imitative of eighteenth century forms, but rather an adaptation of that style to the naturalism and romanticism in art characteristic of the period, 1820-40.

An outstanding feature of the Rococo style was the use of asymmetrical forms. The asymmetry was in considerable contrast to the severity and orthodoxy of classical outlines formerly in vogue. Something of a reaction to Rococo had appeared in the Regency and Empire styles, where emphasis had been laid upon a certain line and formality. In the 1820's and 1830's, potters like Rose at Coalport, the Bramelds at Swinton, and Bloor at Derby, introduced a new and somewhat extravagent freedom of line and decoration to their work. This was *Revived Rococo*.

The style varied in a number of ways; for example, vases were made with three handles instead of the more symmetrical two. The painted decoration of flowers and other subjects was grouped in irregular patterns. Colours were at their best, brilliant; at their worst, garish. Porcelain pieces were very liberally decorated. It seems sometimes that the artists felt they must paint every inch of china, in order to obtain the highest aesthetic effect.

Another feature of Revived Rococo was the extensive use of applied flowers cut out from the paste with a very sharp lancet-like knife, applied to dish or basket, and afterwards glazed and painted in natural colours. Roses, carnations, convolvulus and anemones were favourites at Rockingham. The natural appearance of their work both in shape and colouring, has rarely been equalled. Unfortunately these applied decorations are very fragile, and pieces with all the flowers intact are very rare. The wares are, of course, veritable dust traps, and the frequent washing necessary for those in use or on open display, must have caused much breakage.

The manner of flower and landscape painting was also typical of Revived Rococo. The flowers, butterflies and insects with which the porcelain was decorated, display great exactness and attention to detail. Views were as topographically correct as could be achieved. We may decry this representational art as sad stuff compared with the "freedom" of "action painting", and of abstract forms in general; but it is well to remember that in the early nineteenth century opportunities for seeing the great country seats and cathedrals were strictly limited. Pictures of all kinds were less numerous than they are now, and "a view as near the original as possible" was both fashionable and desirable. It is foolish to deride the past for not being the present; to mock at one's forbears because they did not anticipate our techniques and critical standards. The art of the 1830's and 1840's must be seen within the context of its own time. One prerequisite is what Henry James so aptly termed, "a sense of the past". Knowledge of dates, names and prices is not enough. The atmosphere, the mood of a period, can be apprehended best by reading its popular, but since neglected novels. Let those who condemn the elaborate decoration of Rockingham porcelain pause to reflect that this was an age of lamplight and candlelight, that the tints which seem so bright to us, gaudy even, were softened in rooms gloomy by day and deeply shadowed by night. The golden, the sheened surfaces, would gather what little light there was, and glow upon the sideboard or mantelpiece to eyes less nervous, less electrically strained, than ours...

The Bramelds were, of course, in accord with the artistic concept of the age. Ebenezer Rhodes, an intelligent contemporary, after visiting the pottery in 1826, wrote: "The tea, table and dessert services manufactured at this place are not surpassed in quality, design and execution in any part of the kingdom". But he saw further possibilities in this link between art and industry. "The improvement (of porcelain manufacture)", he continues, "has been rapid, and of national importance: it is nevertheless still capable of greater excellence. In a dessert, tea or table service, the practice of making each article a facsimile of all the others no longer prevails; it may still be further departed from, and perhaps discontinued altogether. The forms of the different services should certainly be alike, and the general character of the paintings selected to adorn them, similar; one thing further is essential. Instead of repeating a rose, a jasmine, or a honeysuckle, the whole garden of Flora might be made to contribute to the ornamenting of this beautiful ware, and the study of botany become a tea-table amusement. If a hundred different articles constituted one set, a hundred different subjects of the same character might be selected. Sets of porcelain might thus be made as instructive as a treatise on botany, illustrated with representations of the most beautiful plants and flowers that Nature produces".

Here breathes a forerunner of the 1851 Exhibition, but Mr. Rhodes has yet to amplify his theme. "The blueware manufactured at the different potteries of the kingdom might at no very great expense include all the best mansions in the kingdom. Chatsworth, Blenheim, Woobourn (*sic*), Castle Howard, etc., would form a series of excellent subjects, and the monastic remains of the country might likewise be made to contribute to the same purpose. This manufacture, great as it has become, has only just passed the stages of infancy, and begun to move. Properly used, fostered and encouraged, it is capable not of being made a source of amusement only, but of useful instruction; and the Rockingham Works at Swinton will, I trust, at no very distant day realise a part at least of those visionary improvements and pleasing anticipations". As Mr. Rhodes was no potter, and wrote the foregoing lines just after his visit to Swinton, it is fair to assume that these ideas had been advanced in conversation with Thomas Brameld himself. Broadly speaking, this was a line the potter intended to take, and ere long the attempt was made.

This then, was the artistic climate when Thomas Brameld, having completed his porcelain experiments, and obtained the Earl's backing, launched the concern on its most ambitious voyage.

*   *   *   *

(b) The Rhinoceros Vases.

One of the first really important pieces of porcelain completed in 1826, was the first of the two "Rhinoceros" vases (Plate VIc). These creations represent the extremity of "Revived Rococo" to which the Rockingham factory went. Because of this they have evoked a good deal of adverse comment, much transferred thoughtlessly and unjustly to the greater part of the firm's products. We feel that one commentator tends to copy another—a common fault with certain historians.

Rhodes, who saw the first vase when newly made in 1826, gives a detailed and enthusiastic description of it. "At the time I visited these works, Messrs. Bramheld (*sic*) and Co. had just finished a large specimen of porcelain ware of the finest quality and the most exquisite workmanship. It is a scent jar forty-four inches in height and nearly a hundred pounds in weight, exclusive of the cover, being all fired and completed in one piece.

"The base or plinth is triangular, with circular projections at the corners from which three paws of the lion rise angularly with curtains between them to support the body of the jar which is globular. The neck is beautifully perforated with hexagonal honey-comb openings for the perfume to escape. (*Upon these three large, but very life-like bees*

99

crawl).[1] Three rustic handles of knotted oak divide the jar into compartments; branches of oak in foliage, intermixed with acorns, rising from the plinth spread tastefully over the curtains and lion's legs, and continue entwined with the handles to the neck, the base of which they encircle. The cover is ornamented with oak branches and foliage to correspond, the whole being surmounted by a beautiful model of a rhinoceros or unicorn of Holy Writ. The three compartments into which the jar is divided are enriched with highly finished paintings by Mr. J. Brameld from the adventures of Don Quixote. These comprise the knight's attack on the army of sheep—his meeting Dulcinea enchanted in the form of a country wench—and the dejected mood in which he travelled on with Sancho after the interview (*Sancho however, is grinning broadly*)—all from designs by Stothard. The circular corners of the pedestal and cover are adorned with six subjects of rare botanical plants accurately drawn and coloured from the originals in the gardens at Wentworth; painted in compartments on a delicate blue ground, intermixed with rich burnished and chased gold ornamental work. The whole of the foliage is burnished or chased gold, and the handles are tastefully formed and relieved with gold". (*Under the circular cover, eight spokes radiate about half-way centre to the circumference. Each of these spokes is painted on both sides, and the back panel of each section is likewise decorated. These partially concealed paintings are copies of the celebrated tail-pieces of T. Bewick, the contemporary wood engraver*).

The vase so meticulously described by Rhodes, is now in the Clifton Park Museum, Rotherham, acquired after the Wentworth House sale. So far as we can ascertain the vase had been at Wentworth since its completion. Whether it was a present from the Bramelds to the Earl as a thank offering for his financial assistance, or whether the Earl bought it (possibly for the £100 indicated in the Estate Accounts) we cannot state with certainty. Its stay, however, at Wentworth was not without incident. Close examination of the vase reveals considerable damage to the main body, which has been repaired though not in a particularly neat or expert fashion. The story goes that one foggy day when hunting was impossible, one or two younger members of the Fitzwilliam family decided upon a romp indoors, and in the course of this frolic, over crashed this superb object of art! The accident is unlikely to have been the result of routine dusting...

*   *   *   *

The second Rhinoceros Vase, now lodged in the Victoria and Albert Museum, London, was acquired by them in 1859, from the well-known china dealers, Messrs. Mortlock for the sum of one hundred guineas. There is no record for whom it was made; the date of manufacture

[1] Italics indicate additional detail by authors.

being recorded as "about 1826"[1] or alternatively 1830. It was certainly made later than the Wentworth Vase, but this is not surprising as in fact, the vases are not a pair. The second differs from that in Rotherham by having the panels decorated by elaborate and vivid flower paintings —the work of Edwin Steel—instead of scenes from *Don Quixote*. These painted panels have dark backgrounds, and each contains an architectural feature—a doorway, a summer-house and a cottage. The base is maroon and bears gilt decoration: sheaved trumpets, flags and spears are discernible. One of the main panels has a screen of grapes painted upon it—a favourite subject of the Steels.[2] The cover is decorated with three floral patterns, but there are no hidden paintings beneath it. The rhinoceros appears to be standing knee-deep in grass (slivers of coloured porcelain). The general effect is of a dark and rather heavy piece. One misses the clear blue background and the clean white porcelain of the Rotherham vase.

The vases have, at one time or another, had a mixed reception from the critics. Llewellyn Jewitt, for his part was unfeignedly enthusiastic. He writes of the one at Wentworth as "the largest china vase ever produced at that time in a single piece in this country . . . one which is of surpassing beauty . . . and exquisitely painted".

John Ward, in *The Potters Art*, 1828, was moved to celebrate in verse—

> *That splendid vase no vulgar hand designed,*
> *Its fabrick shows th' inventive master mind—*

After a further thirty lines of somewhat laboured description the poet concludes—

> *Such various arts in this rare work combine,*
> *Of moulding, carving, painting and design,*
> *As may compete with choicest works of skill,*
> *Which the most fam'd Museum grace and fill.*

Mr. W. B. Honey, writing in *English Pottery and Porcelain* is more critical than lyrical. Dealing with "Revived Rococo" in general, and the Rockingham style in particular, he states, "At its amusing worst its extravagence takes such forms as the two enormous rhinoceros vases . . . with huge paw feet beneath a monstrous body smothered in applied oak leaves and twigs . . . The painting on this vase (that decorated by Steel) is also typical: hot in colour and laboured in handling, but not without a vulgar abundance and excess that reveal an unmistakable vitality if little taste".

[1] Victoria and Albert Museum label.

[2] The Steels, Thomas the father, and his sons, Edwin and Horatio, are referred to in various works as Steele. From the records of the Minton Works and the signature on the tray in Rotherham Museum, the true reading is Steel.

Mr. Ethbert Brand, a former curator of the Clifton Park Museum, was far more scathing. "A mad knight", he said, "tilting at windmills is sanity itself compared to this porcellaneous conception designed by John Wager Brameld in 1826 . . . These vases are examples of everything that should be avoided in the modelling and decoration of porcelain. Restraint and repose is entirely lacking. Brameld had far better kept to his little brown pots".[1]

* * * *

(c) Services.

As we have already contended, it is most unlikely that the Bramelds manufactured porcelain in any quantity before 1826. All the indications are that the Earl's subsidy not only brought them out of their difficulties, but also enabled them to make the advance they were hoping for into full-scale porcelain production. Thus while the rhinoceros vase was being made, the remainder of the factory would be busy with normal earthenware and pottery goods, but increasingly as new building came into use, china would leave the kilns and pass to the decorating rooms to be painted by the newly-arrived artists.

A bewildering array of wares became available for these men to work upon. The list is extensive, and we are conscious that had we tried to present a complete and comprehensive record of all goods made at Swinton, we should still have omitted certain items and types of article. What follows is a general indication of wares, both useful and decorative. We shall describe only those pieces actually seen (and in most cases handled) by us, or whose authenticity cannot be in doubt.

The production of tea, coffee, dinner and dessert services, would engage the bulk of the firm's resources. A good many examples have survived, and many fine pieces can be seen in each of the four main public collections. Anything like a complete service is however, a rarity, and even part services attractively decorated, command good prices.[2]

The factory pattern books still exist and are of primary importance in establishing the authenticity of tea and dessert wares. We have been able to study three of the four books. Each contains both tea and dessert patterns. A quarter section of a dessert plate or saucer is illustrated, and one can thus see the shape and moulding of the piece; the ground colour; the style of decoration; and occasionally the name of the decorating artist. Each pattern is numbered, and the "china tea"

---

[1] From the text of a lecture to the Rotherham Rotary Club, September 23rd, 1925. The address is in the files of the Rotherham Central Library. The vase had not then been secured for the Museum.

[2] We cannot possibly deal with the full range of patterns, designs, shapes, colours and decorations of Rockingham services. We can only indicate general characteristics and illustrate typical examples.

and the dessert patterns have separate numerical sequences. The appropriate numbers were painted upon the underside of the majority of plates and saucers in each service; they appear a little less frequently on tea pots, cream jugs, comports and dishes. On otherwise unmarked wares the authentic pattern number is a reliable aid to identification. Unfortunately, the pattern books do not show the shapes for cups, basins, jugs, pots, comports and dishes.

We may deduce that tea services were offered in over a thousand different patterns. In the first book patterns begin at number 595 and end at 995. The sequence is continued in the two further books until the last pattern is reached at 1559. There can be little doubt that this is the upper limit of Rockingham tea-ware patterns. The lower limit of 595 is not conclusive and further research is needed on this point. At least one tea service (Pattern 568) has been found below the 595 figure, and though this could indicate the use of an earthenware pattern on porcelain, there may be further unrecorded examples of pattern numbers lower than 595 appearing on griffin-marked wares.

Over and above the series 595-1559, a few patterns are given prefixed by the figure 2. These fractional numbers run from 2/17 to 2/78. As some of the pages are loose in this part of the pattern book and the loss of some sheets a possibility, this fractional series could be slightly longer than indicated. Our own observation of the wares makes us confident that 2/100 is the outside limit that could have been reached.

Although over a thousand patterns are given, the number of different *designs* is far fewer than this. Designs were repeated in a variety of different colour combinations, and with very small alterations in flower grouping or similar re-arrangement of decorative detail. The pattern books contain instructions to the workmen—"*764—as for*", and then a standard design number is quoted, "*in glaze kiln blue*" or "*in wood green*", or whatever the variant was. Nor must we presume that all these patterns were actually produced. The pattern book served to indicate to customers the range of the factory's output. Quite a substantial proportion of patterns may never have been ordered. Generally speaking, the higher the pattern number the later the ware, however, this cannot be taken as an invariable rule. It must be borne in mind that an early pattern—say 665—could still be ordered in the closing years of the Pottery's life.

The dessert service patterns begin at number 450 in the first book and continue to 875 in the other books. Here again the upper limit is more definite than the lower, but in this case we have not encountered a marked service with a number lower than 433.

Unmarked tea and dessert wares with pattern numbers as high as seven or eight thousand have often been proclaimed to us as genuine Rockingham wares. Now that the limits can be more firmly indicated it is to be hoped that such attributions will cease. If access could be

103

gained to the fourth pattern book which is reputed to be the earliest and to contain earthenware patterns, complete precision would be brought to an important topic which until recently has been either shrouded in ignorance or wildly speculative.

Service plates are almost invariably of the same general design. They have a coloured decorative border, usually outlined in gilt, or with panels for floral or scenic paintings; there is then an area of unpainted ware, sometimes very small indeed, and in the centre of the plate further decoration—a landscape, a flower cluster or a single specimen, a country seat, a coat-of-arms, a bird, or merely a gilt motif. These are, in fact, similar to the plates made by most of the important factories. The Bramelds were great copyists, and in this aspect of their work display little originality (Plate Vb).

But Rockingham services do possess a number of features worthy of special note. The gilt is lavish and of a good durable quality, though with the passage of time it tends to acquire a coppery tint. The views on many services are entirely imaginary, or, if real, are only of local significance. When a definite building or landscape is displayed, the piece is usually marked. Sometimes this is done in gilt letters just below the painting, otherwise the description is on the reverse side.

The more expensive services, most of which were directly commissioned, would be painted by the senior artists. Periodically in the pattern book one reads, "Flowers by Steel" pencilled in the blank centre of the plate. Other patterns are marked, "Flowers by Ll . . . g" (Llandeg). The purchasers of less costly services, would one presumes, have to be content with, "Flowers by girls". The flowers portrayed however, were real and not infrequently rare and exotic. A number of very fine paintings of the highest standard have survived. Edwin Steel was responsible for several excellent pieces. Most of these have an undecorated but moulded rim, usually a primrose leaf pattern with the entire centre of the plate given over to the painting (Plate IIIb). Steel, as might be expected, specialised in flower and fruit studies, and examples of his work can be seen in the Rotherham Museum and in the Victoria and Albert. Speight, was another artist who worked on highly decorative plates. Invariably, these were signed by him, and it seems likely that the work was done away from the factory. Mrs. Llewellyn has a fine study by Speight of women bathing ("The Enchanted Stream, Speight *pinxit*."), and Mr. Redfern has also a signed plate in his collection ("The Bridesmaid", after Lawrence).

Another particularly attractive kind of plate is very similar to that noted earlier when dealing with earthenware. These are painted with studies of flowers, and plants, delineated much in the style of Collinson. The names of the flowers—in English—are in gold on the back of the plates. Mrs. Llewellyn has a number of these masterly pieces in her collection.

The Pottery had much talent to draw upon. The better among the artists painted freehand, producing pictures of great naturalness and vivacity. The less talented worked to transferred outlines, usually in black,[1] but even so, their work is fresh and colourful, a delight to the eye. When one considers the price paid for mediocre paintings on canvas, the few pounds a finely enamelled Rockingham plate costs is a trifling sum. The owner of such a plate has a miniature picture framed in porcelain, which can give every bit as much pleasure as the most costly of artistic status symbols.

It is not only for the enamelled decoration and gilding that Rockingham services have won repute. Their ground colours are particularly fine, and many enthusiasts believe that they have never been surpassed by any other English factory. The range and clarity of these colours—greens, blues and reds predominating—is outstanding. The pattern book lists seven varieties of green: bailey green—wood green—French green—chrome green—yellow green—olive green—and raseberry (sic) green. Of blues, there were Brunswick blue—biscuit and purple.

The purple is really a deep Royal blue very similar in shade to that used by both Derby and Worcester, but the other two shades are not encountered to the same extent. The light blue is akin to Cambridge blue. The deeper tone is a glorious cobalt blue with a matt finish. A "wet blue" it was once termed—an excellent description as one half expects one's fingers to be marked after handling.

The range of red shades is equally wide though only three are named —pink, crimson and maroon; the first of these being the delicate rose pink. Yellow too was sometimes used as a ground colour in a rather subdued tone, easily distinguishable from the bright canary yellow of Derby. This may have been the "yellow green" which is mentioned. Other colours in this range are buff, "stone", and a curious combination "(glaze kiln) drab light buff". It is, of course, extremely difficult to visualise the shades some of these terms indicate, but we give the full list exactly as pencilled in the pattern book. Incidentally the water colour painting in the pattern book is not a great help in discrimination, as the shades differ considerably from the final result on the porcelain.

One other colour deserves notice. Tea services with a grey ground and gilt ornamentation are much sought after. The subdued tones of the grey are more readily acceptable to modern taste than the exuberance of purple or maroon. Produced probably during the latter years of the Pottery's life when debts were once more darkening the horizon, and economies were being made amongst the artist staff, these services are as tasteful as anything ever produced at Swinton. Their restrained elegance disproves the oft repeated and much too glib assertion, that Rockingham porcelain is "vulgar", and its decoration excessive. It has

[1] Coalport transfer outlines are invariably in pink—a useful aid to identification.

been stated that the grey ground was introduced especially to satisfy Quaker customers, who found other Rockingham colours too ostentatious for their taste; but whether the decoration was adjusted to a moral and spiritual purpose or not, such a service is delightful to behold, to live with and to use. Many similar services were produced either in grey or in green with admirably restrained gilding. The intense whiteness, and the general excellence of the Rockingham paste is shown to great advantage in such pieces. These simple designs attracted the attention of other potteries, who imitated (Coalport is a case in point), so that today such wares are frequently offered for sale as unmarked "Rockingham". Even these are far superior to the products of later nineteenth century potteries, who in quest of good patterns, have turned to those of the Bramelds. Pieces can be seen marked, "Rockingham reproduction"—Litherlands, Bold St., Liverpool." (Litherlands were china retailers).

Certain other features of service decoration and design call for notice. Services were made in which the tea cups and saucers were modelled in the shape of sea shells. These, while elegant enough, were somewhat impractical. As very few examples can be found, one may assume that they were not turned out in quantity. (The V. and A. has a good specimen, so has Rotherham Museum, the Yorkshire Museum piece is marked). Another interesting feature is in the decoration to be found inside quite a number of tea and coffee cups. A view was painted at the bottom of the cup, and examples are known of cups with two or more pictures on the inside walls. Such decoration, delicately achieved, must, on account of the additional time required for painting, have added considerably to the cost (Plate IVa).

A number of motifs, though not exclusive to the Swinton factory, appear with great regularity in pattern after pattern. Scallop edges and gadroon are frequent, so too is the moulded shell motif on the edge of plates, dishes and comports. Great use is made of the vine leaf and grapes design—usually fringed by a looped and trailing tendril, an adaptation of the familiar Wedgwood pattern. The seaweed pattern of tendril-like fronds, mostly in gilt, is another favourite decoration. It is worth stressing that other potters decorated their wares with these motifs, and used moulds which are similar to Rockingham shapes. The features indicated are merely a guide to authentic identification— not conclusive proof of it.

The dishes and comports in dessert and dinner services are variously designed and liberally decorated. Four or five views or sprays of flowers, and sometimes many more, are to be found painted on one piece. The gilding is rich, and sometimes heavy, and the shapes of the pieces well-varied and often extremely intricate.

In tea and coffee services, the sugar basins, cream jugs and tea pots, are usually most elegant. The pots are well shaped for their purpose, and though some of the basins and milk jugs have a simple outline, others are both more elaborate and more heavily decorated. The designs for these articles have a number of origins, including the obvious Chinese influence; but the chief source of inspiration seems to have been in the craftsmanship of the silversmith. It is difficult to trace whether the Bramelds copied silver-work patterns directly—was Wentworth used here?—or whether they based their designs on those of other potteries using silverware models. The proximity of Sheffield to the Rockingham works suggests one relationship. Unfortunately, it would appear that no pattern book or design sketches for these items have survived. It was the normal practice for services to have two cups to each saucer—one usually flat and wide for tea the other more upright and "modern" in shape for coffee. Side plates as we know them were not part of the service.

If the Rhinoceros vases may be said to represent the peak of one aspect of the Bramelds art, then the Royal Dessert Service is another. Jewitt states that he possessed the original pen-and-ink sketches, dated 12th November, 1830, and signed "per J.W.B." (John Wager Brameld). Subsequently, in his account of the pottery Jewitt writes that the comports were all designed by Thomas Brameld. Presumably the pen-and-ink sketches were all of the various sample plates (and possibly contained suggestions for the general form of the comports). At any rate the two men seem to have had it between them. When the royal favour had been bestowed, Thomas took control and assumed direct responsibility for the production. Unfortunately we have been unable to trace the present whereabouts of these sketches.

The service itself is a remarkable piece of work. Retained at Buckingham Palace, it is still used on important state occasions. Although it has never been on public display, we have had the good fortune to see a number of lantern slides of several of the pieces taken a few years ago by Mr. Lewis Brameld. These photographs give some indication of the superb workmanship and artistry embodied in the service; copies are in Rotherham Museum. The full service display must look remarkable in the appropriate setting of a state banquet.

Some idea of the opulent nature of the service can be gained by examining specimen plates and comports, several of which are still in existence, and on display in public galleries. The Victoria and Albert Museum has two such plates: one with oak leaves applied in gilt over a green background; the other having a lattice work pattern and oak leaves in gilt, has a pale blue ground. Both plates are marked, and were presented to the Museum by the 5th Earl Fitzwilliam, having formerly been in Wentworth House. Several plates are in the Royal Worcester Porcelain Factory Museum, and Earl Fitzwilliam has retained in his own collection, several of the pattern or specimen plates of various designs. (The Earl's collection contains a number of outstanding pieces which were specially made for Wentworth House). The Yorkshire Museum, York, has a plate which unfortunately is damaged; while Mr. Redfern has an excellent specimen in his collection of the pattern which was selected by the King. Plate IIIa shows the copy in Clifton Park Museum. Mr. W. Mason, of Rotherham owns an interesting plate in a partially completed state. Obviously it was discarded before work on it had proceeded very far. Another piece of the service, or of a similar service, can be seen at the Weston Park Museum, Sheffield. This is a comport ornamented with guava fruit. The Museum acquired the comport which was in a damaged condition in 1910 from a private collector in Rotherham. It is just possible that this piece was damaged at the factory, and set aside, or sold to a private person. On the other hand it may be from a service made for a foreign monarch, who (like the Duchess of Cumberland) had asked for the comports to be the same as those of His Majesty. It is decorated with views of Raby Castle, Durham, and of Netherby, Cumberland. The mark, which is printed twice in purple has the griffin and "Rockingham Works Brameld, Manufacturer to the King, Queen and Royal Family". In York Museum is one of the more elaborate three-tier comports, each plate encrusted with applied coloured flowers on the rim, the whole piece surmounted by a basin, which like the base of the comport is decorated with fine paintings. As with the piece in the Sheffield Museum, its exact origin is somewhat obscure. (See Appendix a, p. 141).

The service was originally supposed to consist of 200 pieces—12 dozen plates and 56 larger items. When Mr. Brameld (to whom we are indebted for a good deal of information about the Royal Service) visited the Palace, he was given a list indicating the present extent of the service. Of the original 144 plates, 119 are now fit for use. Of the larger items the full total as used at present seems to be 62 or even 64, not 56 as usually stated. The details supplied to Mr. Brameld have recently been checked by us, and the Master of the Household kindly supplied the list printed below—

Description	Size (height)	Number of Items
Three-tier compotier	22-in.	8
Two-tier compotier	19-in.	4
Cake comports (sheaf of corn stem)	9-in.	8
Dessert comports (pineapple stem)	10½-in.	4
Dessert comports (blackberry stem)	9¾-in.	3
Dessert comports (oyster coral-shell)	7-in.	4
Ice Pails or chalices (In Warwick Style) ...	13-in.	7
Dessert comport on tree supporters with basket pattern bowl	12-in.	8

Description	Size (height)	Number of Items
Small decorative pieces, vases	7½-in.	8
Decorative fruit comports (continental fruit sprays)	9-in.	8

It seems possible that a blackberry stem comport, and one of the ice-pails has been broken or lost, as all the pieces are in sets of 4 or 8. The discrepancy in numbers seems to be accounted for by the 8 "small decorative pieces—vases". Almost certainly these were not part of the original service, and have been included in the Palace records because they are customarily used with the full dessert service. It is not known how the additional pieces came to be added to the original 200.

The plates are identical to the one illustrated; the ground colour a pale blue. The painting of the royal coat-of-arms and the "St. George and Dragon" motif, is wonderfully executed. The time taken to complete the painting, and the quantity of gilt lavished upon the plates, would make Thomas Brameld's estimate of £12 a plate ludicrously low. One imagines that each plate must have cost at least twice that amount to produce.

The larger pieces are quite remarkable, particularly the three-tier comportier which are topped with a basin or dish. All the larger items are decorated with paintings, many of which depict country seats or other places of historical or topographical interest. In some cases the artists may well have visited scenes to make preliminary sketches, though obviously the more distant would be copied from published prints and other illustrations. A number of the pictures are copies of well-known allegorical paintings of figure studies. The clarity and brilliance of the enamels, the skill of the artists in reducing to such a small compass, and the masssive opulence of the gilding, are features which cannot but excite admiration.

The large pieces are decorated in a manner indicative of their function. Thus the shell-fish comports have a wonderful red, coral-like stem, and the basket is decorated with the most realistically shaped and coloured sea-shells. The cake or biscuit comports, are decorated with sheaves of corn and finely modelled ears of wheat; and four of the fruit comports have a finely modelled pineapple as a support to the dish. The other pieces are similarly decorated, so that naturalism and artistry are combined to a remarkable degree.

A fair number of the factory's leading artists had a hand in the decoration of the service. John Wager Brameld certainly painted parts of it; so did William Corden. Haigh Hirstwood and his sons, William and Joseph are also recorded as having been engaged on the work. Isaac Baguley was doubtless responsible for much of the gilding. As for the rest wc can only assume that in a work of such complexity, the united skills of many would be necessary to complete the successful masterpiece.

The service must have cost the Bramelds more than the £5,000 they received for it. Unfortunately we have not been able to trace any document setting forth a detailed account of the complete transaction. Tradition maintains that expenditure was over double the contract price. One wonders how much of the excess was due to discarding imperfect pieces at various stages of manufacture. The Bramelds were noted as perfectionists. Every piece of the Royal service would have to conform to the highest standards—in short, to be fit for a king!

The dessert service was not the only royal contract fulfilled by the Bramelds. We have already mentioned commissions from the King of the Belgians, the Duchess of Cumberland and the Duke of Sussex. It is not generally known that a breakfast service was made for William IV's wife, Queen Adelaide. We have no details of the size of this service, or when it was made and delivered. In style it is in complete contrast to the elaborate dessert service. The saucers and plates have a border of simple design; the only other decoration is a crown with monogram A.R. (Adelaide Regina) in the centre of each piece. It is marked with the griffin and the words, "Rockingham Works Brameld, Manufacturer to the King". A cup and saucer from this stylish service can be seen in the Sheffield Museum; the Victoria and Albert also has a plate. The Bramelds portrayed their royal patrons on certain wares. In the Yorkshire Museum are two fine plates each with a maroon and gold decorated border, the centre of one bearing a portrait of King William IV and the other that of his Queen. It is recorded that a number of pattern plates were prepared in 1837 for submission to Queen Victoria when it was hoped to gain further royal recognition by alterations to the dessert service. One of these plates is in private hands. From the photographs we have seen of it, there is no doubt that it was a fine piece of work; but the young Queen (or her advisers) decided against further expenditure.

We take a long stride in moving from the elaborate and costly royal services, to the miniature or toy tea-sets manufactured at the Rockingham Works. These tiny sets are attractive and much sought after. They were made in a variety of sizes, beginning with cream jugs and basins less than an inch in height, to small teapots as much as three inches high. The most commonly found pieces are teacups and saucers, teapots, kettles and cream jugs. Most that we have seen are very similar in style to the products of the Coalport factory, and decorated with small coloured flowers and buds applied to the pieces in typically rococo fashion. Other specimens have shown flowers painted on a coloured ground. Some good examples of these pleasant trifles are to be seen at both the Sheffield and Rotherham museums.

PLATE XIII

a. Earthenware dish, transfer printed in light blue with the "Floral Sketches" pattern. 18½in. × 15in. (BRAMELD +1 *impressed*, and *Floral Sketches Granite China*, printed). *Mr. and Mrs. P. R. Helm.*

b. Porcelain dessert plate, shell and gadroon moulded edge. Enamelled flowers and gilding. Diam. 9½in. (Red griffin, printed). *T. A. Lockett.*

c. Porcelain dessert plate, detailed moulding on rim outlined in gilt, enamelled flowers. Diam. 9½in. (Puce griffin mark.) *Mr. and Mrs. P. R. Helm.*

PLATE XIV

a.   Porcelain tureen stand with rustic handles, decorated with an enamel painting of Wentworth Wodehouse, the seat of Earl Fitzwilliam. 9¾in. × 7½in. (Unmarked, see text). *Mr. and Mrs. A. A. Eaglestone.*

b.   Porcelain cups: (*top left*) Pattern 665 (red griffin); (*top right*) Pattern 833 (puce griffin); (*bottom left*) Pattern 656 (red griffin); (*bottom right*) Pattern 1161 (puce griffin). Saucers only marked. *T. A. Lockett.*

Two further points are worth noting. In common with all the great potteries, the Rockingham works was influenced by the ceramic art of China. The Cadogan pot, and the influence of oriental designs upon the shape of teapots, sugar basins, etc., has already been noted. Chinese influence is also directly displayed in the designs and decorative patterns adopted for some of the Rockingham services. Chinese scenes appear on the porcelain and earthenware sometimes as underglaze blue transfer printed patterns decorated with gilt, or bright red and green enamels are used as overglaze in typically oriental designs. A feature of this latter type of decoration is that it usually appears on octagonal plates, a shape of which we have never encountered in Rockingham porcelain except in association with a Chinese pattern. These octagonal plates are very rare, and because they are so different from the normal Brameld style rather difficult to identify if unmarked. We presume that full services were made, but we cannot recall having seen other than plates and soup dishes in this style. (See Appendix b, p. 141).

A full list of the marks used on Rockingham services is given, but one point is worth stressing. It is often stated that Rockingham services are rarely marked. This impression has been created because so much good-quality, but unmarked, nineteenth century china has been wrongly attributed to Rockingham. The Coalport and Spode enterprises—to name only two—were the makers of a considerable quantity of unmarked tableware, now erroneously ascribed to Rockingham. Even mid and late nineteenth century china from some of the many "Staffordshire" potteries can be seen labelled "Rockingham". We have often been shown, or seen illustrated in general works, tea services, purporting to be Rockingham, which clearly were not made at Swinton. Such wares, generally decorated in green, or grey, and gold in a style similar to the Rockingham style, are mid-nineteenth century products, made at potteries such as G. F. Bowers & Co. or S. Alcock & Co. A number of such wares correctly ascribed are illustrated by Mr. G. A. Godden in his recent book, "*British Pottery and Porcelain 1780-1850*". This work and Mr. Godden's other studies shed light on this topic, and clarify many misconceptions. (See Appendix c, p. 141).

It is worth reiterating that a goodly proportion of genuine Rockingham tableware was marked. Tea and coffee services bear the griffin mark on the saucers, rarely on the teapots, basins and cream jugs, though these latter items often carry the pattern number. Dessert services have the griffin mark on the plates and often on the dishes; the comports are marked less frequently. A study of the *exact* forms, shapes, decoration and markings of the genuine wares is the best way to separate the Swinton products from later "Rockingham style" wares.

As we have already suggested, the production of services would probably have occupied the bulk of the factory's resources, but other products—Rockingham figures, Rockingham vases and many ornamental items are from their quality held in high esteem. It is to a short survey of these wares that we now turn.

* * * *

(d) Vases.

Vases, urns, jars and beakers tend to be better cared for, and are thus less prone to damage than other porcelain items. This may be one survival factor. It may be that a proportionally large quantity was made. In any case a goodly number of Rockingham vases have survived to the present day. Many different sizes and patterns were made, and the style of decoration varies considerably from piece to piece.

The rhinoceros vases were the largest and most ambitious of this type of vessel made at Swinton, but many other excellent, if less spectacular pieces were fashioned. These range from spill vases less than 4-in. in height, to the "Dragon" vases described by Jewitt which were 3-ft. 4-in. tall. The latter were so called because the cover was surmounted by a gilt dragon, the handles too being moulded in this form. We have been unable to trace the present whereabouts of these pieces.

In fact, animals and birds frequently provided a motif on Rockingham vases. Though few are to be found with pictures of animals and birds (John Randall is known to have painted some during his relatively short stay at Swinton, Plate Va) many were modelled with animals or birds as handles. The most commonly seen are decorative vases with gilt handles in the form of a bird's neck and beak. Some models display a beak so long that a gannet, a pelican, or even a curlew, is the bird that springs most to mind. In the Sheffield Museum are two fine vases, the ground colour is green with gold ornamentation, and each has in the panel a superbly painted Italian view, one of Verona, and the other, Isola Bella Lago Maggiore. Jewitt records a set of three vases in green and gold painted with Italian scenes, the two named above, and a third of Bellagio, Lago di Come. The pieces which were then in "the late Mr. Bagshawe's collection", may well be—the third of course missing—those now in Weston Park. It is also a tenable supposition that the painting was executed by Cowen, the Rotherham artist, who is known to have visited Italy.

Covers were also ornamented with models of animals, flowers, birds and butterflies; the rhinoceros and dragon vases are typical examples, and some excellent beakers and vases were made with monkeys on the cover. Hexagonal in shape, and decorated in the Chinese style, these beakers usually have alternate panels with Oriental designs. "Monkey" beakers and jars are much sought after by collectors, but alas, are rarely found. Mrs. Llewellyn has a fine collection of hexagonal jars with pink, maroon and dark blue ground colours. One matching set of

112

five in dark blue must be unique. (These were illustrated in the *Connoisseur Year Book, 1962*). Butterflies modelled on covers were usually painted in natural colours rather than in gilt like the monkeys and other animals. Only a small proportion of vases and jars had covers, but a great many pieces originally having a cover are now without, since that part of the ornament was most accident-prone.

The shapes of the larger vases varied. A few of the styles display the over-elaboration into which the Bramelds were led by an effort to out-shine their rivals at Derby and Coalport. Thomas Brameld may (to use Jewitt's words) have been a "man of exquisite taste", but occasionally he was guilty of mistaking elaborate decoration for good design.

The urn-shaped pot-pourri vases are generally very elegant, some of the most attractive being those modelled with the Warwick style handles. A pair of urns in Rotherham Museum are masterpieces of their kind, with uncoloured applied flowers, and two panels of sparsely painted ones (Plate VIIb). The comparatively large area of undecorated porcelain of the highest quality, beautifully glazed, adds to the attraction of these fine pieces.

One frequently sees vases with elaborately scrolled rococo handles and feet ascribed to Rockingham. It is worth noting that none such that we have seen has been marked with the griffin. In the opinion of a number of experts and experienced collectors these vases belong to Coalport, Grainger-Lee (Worcester), Mintons and other, less well-known potteries, such as S. Alcock & Co. of Burslem.

Apart from the monkey vases, the decoration of the larger Rockingham items was in the factory's typical style. The usual green, blue or red ground colours were applied, and panels left on each side of the vase for paintings, which followed the normal lines of either named or imaginary views, or flower studies. Occasionally—as we have indicated — birds were depicted. Vases which are attributed to Edwin Steel are often characterised by rich dark hues in the flowers and fruit. Steel also seemed to prefer an all-round decorative band to paint on in preference to the panel. Several vases attributed to this artist can be seen in the V. & A. Applied flowers, usually coloured, but sometimes left in the white, were a feature of the more expensive and ambitious productions. So too was the gilding which tended to be lavish during the more prosperous periods in the factory's fortunes.

Special mention must be made of spill vases, which many enthusiasts consider to be among the finest and most stylish of Rockingham wares (Plate Va). Certainly, many fine sets were made. A set of three in apple green, wonderfully painted and flawlessly shaped can be seen in Rotherham Museum. Mr. W. Mason has a beautiful vase about 5-in. high, on a square plinth, the ground colour is green; on the panel an arresting picture of a magpie. Views, flower and fruit compositions, sea shells as well as birds formed the main subjects. Mr. M. Redfern has a pair of spill vases with a delicately depicted strawberry plant covering the whole body of the piece. A similar vase can be seen in the Rotherham Museum (Plate VIIIb). A large maroon spill vase in Mrs. Eaglestone's collection has a fruit composition, which though not in his grandest manner, seems to bear the touch of Edwin Steel. Mrs. Llewellyn's collection contains many fine sets of vases as well as a number of outstanding single pieces.

Five principal shapes of spill vase can be identified. They are: the upright or cylindrical; a rather squat cylindrical vase with ring-shaped handles which is set upon a square plinth; two forms with an out-curving lip; and the full-lipped or "mushroom" shape. The two first seem to have been made in two different sizes, the three latter shapes in three sizes.

The collector who possesses a set of spill vases, or even a single one, is fortunate, for all the virtues of Rockingham can be seen there. The clean, white—but warm—porcelain, the excellent clear ground colours, and the delightfully executed small paintings, show to advantage. The nature of the vase precludes over-elaboration.

It is appropriate at this point to mention an interesting fact concerning the identification of vases and other decorative items. A considerable number of pieces many of them marked with the griffin, but some without, have written on the base, often in gold or red, the letters "Cl" followed by a number. The series seems to run from "Cl I" to "Cl 14", at least we have not encountered any number higher than this. A very few pieces have been noted where the mark has simply been "C", followed by a number (C1, C2, and C3 have been seen). The true significance of the mark is rather vague. The most likely explanation is that the mark is that of the gilder. We have never seen it on a piece not decorated with gilt, though it appears, on figures for example, when the only decoration is gilding. The particular importance of this gilder's mark is that, to the best of our knowledge, it is unique to the Rockingham factory. Not all Rockingham decorative pieces bear the mark, but where there is no griffin, a piece bearing the "Cl" mark can be positively identified as Rockingham. The lack of such a mark, does not, however, mean that the piece cannot be a Rockingham product.

Rockingham ornamental items did not carry a conventional pattern number as did the wares of many potteries, though one has often seen unmarked pieces ascribed to Rockingham bearing such numbers. From our observations we are convinced that the majority of Rockingham vases, especially spill vases *were* griffin-marked. This we realise is contrary to accepted notions, but, by and large, we have found that the unmarked wares formerly attributed to Rockingham were in fact made elsewhere. For example, wares bearing the diamond-shaped registration mark can be seen ascribed to Rockingham. The Design

Registration Mark was introduced in 1842—*after* the Bramelds had ceased to manufacture. Thus pieces bearing the mark, either impressed or printed, cannot be Rockingham.

*   *   *   *

(e) Baskets.

There are four principal types of basket which deserve particular reference, the most characteristically Rockingham being the cake baskets. Usually rectangular in shape and fairly shallow, they have features of especial interest. The handles are fashioned in the manner of criss-cross twigs; in the better examples the twigs are attractively delineated in gold. Around the edges of the basket it is usual to find a continuous border of raised and sometimes coloured flowers.

Equally characteristic is the painting in the centre of the basket. In all the marked examples we have seen the central picture has been of a named country house, or similar building. For example, Mrs. Thompson of Rawmarsh, has a basket in her collection with a representation of the North Lodge, St. Leonards. Sprotbro' Rectory is featured on another basket; so are Newstead Abbey, Salisbury Cathedral and Castle Howard. And of course, Wentworth House and Chatsworth were frequently depicted. A fine example of a decorated basket is in the Rotherham Museum. Appropriately the painting is of Clifton House, the former residence of Samuel Walker, the Masbro' ironmaster —Clifton House is now the Rotherham Borough Museum (Plate VIa). Baskets with simpler and probably more sturdy handles were made; and so were pieces without applied flowers on the rim. Circular baskets with the crossed twig handles and raised flowers are found more rarely (Plate VIIIa).

An attractive and very rare type of basket is shaped in the form of large leaves, the piece glazed in white condition except that the veins of the leaves are slightly raised and picked out in gold. The looped handle has touches of gilt. These baskets appear to have been made in two, or possibly three, sizes. There is a fine example in Sheffield Museum.

The third type is not really a basket at all, but a sweet-meat dish, or possibly a pin tray. In appearance however, these are like small scale replicas of the cake-baskets. Cross twig handles are usual, an interior painting, frequently a view, though sometimes a flower or a butterfly, is nearly always to be found; and though these trifles are rarely more than 4-in. square, applied flower buds decorate a number. York Museum has certain good examples.

Posy bowls were sometimes modelled as baskets. With a circular base, a pastoral scene painted continuously round the main body of the bowl; the covers pierced with holes for flowers, and the whole

115

lifted by a handle, these most attractive trifles look far more like small baskets than flower vases (Plate VIIIa).

A deep basket with blue sides and a rim heavily encrusted with large, gaily-coloured flowers is often ascribed to Rockingham. No specimen with the Rockingham mark has come to our notice, and the pattern book of the Grainger-Lee factory seems to indicate that the baskets were made at Worcester.

*   *   *   *

(f) Cottages and Castles.

Several of the leading potteries in the early 19th century made castles, cottages and churches in pottery and porcelain. Some of these pieces were purely ornamental; others were for use as pastille burners, night-light shelters, money boxes, pipe-racks and inkpots.

There was a time, some years ago, when practically all porcelain cottages were ascribed to Rockingham; but greater knowledge has led to a more sensible assessment of the factory's *possible* output. It is now widely realised that many Staffordshire potteries produced these pieces in china for a good number of years after the Swinton Works had closed, as well as during its lifetime. Even so at least fifty different models of cottages, castles and churches have been attributed to Rockingham, entirely on stylistic grounds. The most esteemed being the mauve cottages and those with applied coloured flowers.

One of the barriers to positive identification is the lack of marked specimens. So far as we are aware none of the cottages ascribed to Rockingham is marked. Certainly there are no marks on any in public collections. Nor have we seen any marked pieces in private hands. It can fairly be asked whether the Swinton factory made any cottages at all. Expert opinion is divided on the matter. "Show me a marked cottage or castle and then I will believe that it is a genuine Rockingham piece", was the comment of one such expert. On the other hand there is a long tradition among dealers and museum authorities that such pieces were made; articles on the subject have appeared in *The Connoisseur* (1912, 1917 and 1918), and certainly the paste and style of decoration of pieces (say in Rotherham Museum) is not inconsistent with having been made at Swinton. Nevertheless, Jewitt makes no mention of cottages and castles, save for one passing reference to a mould of the Keep of Conisboro' Castle, and it is not until the early years of the present century that attributions multiply. The *Connoisseur* articles undoubtedly provided a stimulus. Illustrations accompanying the articles depict "Rockingham" cottages, but it is clearly stated that none is marked. And it is to this fact that we are constantly driven. Despite popular belief to the contrary the Bramelds marked a considerable proportion of their decorative wares. Why did they so conspicuously refrain from attaching their imprint to cottages and castles?

116

It cannot be that they were ashamed to acknowledge their wares, for those attributed to them are the finest. What other reason could they have had? We cannot pretend to answer this question. More detailed research is needed on the whole problem, and until positive conclusions are reached it would be wise to keep an open mind on the subject.

It would indeed be ironical if the Rockingham enterprise had gained a high reputation for a ware it had never produced!

*　　*　　*　　*

(g) Figures.

This is not an easy topic, the chief problem that of correct identification and authentication. As is often the case, a great many of the figures of the less well-known potteries have been passed off as Rockingham. The real difficulty is to draw a line between the genuine and the spurious.

There can be no doubt that the Pottery made some very fine figures both coloured and in the 'biscuit'. We have made a thorough study of as many figures as we could locate, as a result we have been able to establish that a series of 120 marked figures was made. We have not by any means seen all of the 120, in fact some of the figures may now be extinct, others projected, but no moulds made for them. All the figures in the series bear an impressed mould number in addition to the griffin mark. The highest number noted is No. 120, and it is from this that the extent of the series has been deduced.

The decoration of the figures varies. Certain models always seem to have been glazed and coloured, others are invariably in the biscuit state, whilst a number can be found in both media.

The term 'biscuit' indicates that the wares were modelled and fired, but then left in the biscuit state, that is, they were neither glazed nor enamelled. The biscuit state leaves the piece with a dead white, matt finish, and the paste in this state looks chalky and brittle. It is easily dirtied and not so easily cleaned. In this, as in other respects it differs from "parian" ware which superficially it resembles, and with which it is sometimes confused. Parian ware was first produced about 1844, and enjoyed great popularity for many years thereafter. The surface of parian though not shiny like that of a glazed piece, is much less permeable than biscuit, and consequently is much easier to keep clean. Biscuit also differs from parian in that the latter when chipped shows a smooth glass-like surface indicative of its "hard" porcelain nature; whereas biscuit exhibits the typically granulated surface of bone china and of the various "soft" porcelain pastes. The Derby Pottery had been making biscuit ware for many years, and it is quite likely that former Derby employees were responsible for a number of Rockingham biscuit figures. Certainly the Derby influence is plainly discernible.

Of the marked series of 120 figures over 60 have been identified and listed. This list of figures has been compiled by Mr. G. N. Dawnay of Cardiff. We are extremely grateful to him for allowing us to publish it for the first time (The figures marked with an asterisk have been noted by the authors, and are additional to Mr. Dawnay's original list).

ROCKINGHAM BISCUIT AND GLAZED FIGURES AND THEIR MOULD NUMBERS

DESCRIPTION	TYPE OF MARK	GILDER'S MARK	MOULD NUMBER
A Drunk: "Steady Lads". (gl.)	Red, printed		No. 1
A Shepherd and Dog, ⎱ (A pair,	Red, printed		No. 4
A Shepherdess and Sheep. ⎰ both gl.)	and Imp.	Cl.2.	
Madam Vestris in "Buy a Broom" (gl.)	Red, printed.		No. 6
John Liston as "Simon Pengander". (gl.)	Red, printed		No. 7
John Liston as "Paul Pry". (gl.)	Red, printed		No. 9
John Liston as "Lubin Log". (gl.)	Red, printed		No. 11
"Paysanne du Mangfall en Tirol".	Imp.		No. 15
"Paysanne du Canton de Zurich". (gl.)	Imp.		No. 18
*"Paysanne des Environs de Bilbao".	Imp.		No. 21
"Paysanne de Sagan en Tirol". (gl.)	Imp.	Cl.2.	No. 22
*Boy with a Knapsack, ⎱ (A pair,	Imp.		No. 23
*Girl with a bundle of Faggots. ⎰ both bisc.)			
Turkish Gentleman. (gl.)	Imp.		No. 25
Boy with a Pitcher, ⎱ (A pair,	Imp.		No. 26
Girl with a Pitcher ⎰ both gl.)			
Boy seated writing, ⎱ (A pair)	Imp.		No. 28
Girl seated sewing. ⎰			
A Toper. (gl.)	Imp.		No. 29
*Girl with a basket of Flowers.	Imp.		No. 31
Beggar Boy, ⎱ (A pair)	Imp.		No. 36
Beggar Girl. ⎰			
*Boy with a basket of Eggs. (gl.)	Imp.	Cl.2.	No. 36
A Pilgrim. (gl.)	Imp.		No. 37
The Whistling Cobbler.	Unmk.	C.3.	No. 39
*Kneeling Boy feeding a Dog.	Imp.		No. 40
Kneeling Boy feeding a Rabbit, (A ⎱ Imp.			No. 44
*A Girl with a Sheep. pair) ⎰ Unmk.			No. 44
"Paysan de la Vallee der Ziller en Tirol". (gl.)	Imp.	Cl.2.	No. 50
"Paysan du Canton de Zurich".	Imp.		No. 53

DESCRIPTION	TYPE OF MARK	GILDER'S MARK	MOULD NUMBER
Paysan Piedmontais de la Vallee d'Aoste (gl.)	Imp.		No. 57
Shepherd leaning on a crook with a dog and a sheep.	Imp.		No. 58
Sleeping Child.	Imp.		No. 63
Awakening Child.	Imp.		No. 64
*Sleeping Child	Imp.		No. 65
A very small group of a Rabbit and Young.	Unmk.		No. 70
A very small sitting Dog. (gl.)	Unmk.	*Cl*.1.	No. 71
A very small Rabbit. (gl.)	Unmk.		No. 72
A very small Squirrel. (gl.)	Unmk.	*Cl*.1.	No. 73
A very small sitting Dog. (gl.)	Unmk.	*Cl*.1.	No. 74
A Pug Dog. (gl.)	Imp.		No. 76
A Cat sitting on a Cushion. (gl.)	Imp.		No. 77
A Stag lying down, ⎫ (A pair, A Hind lying down. ⎭ both gl.)	Imp.	*Cl*.2.	No. 80
A Dog running. (gl.)	Imp.	*Cl*.1.	No. 83
"Homme du Peuple a Valence".	Imp.		No. 84
*A Dog lying down, head raised. (gl.)	Imp.	*Cl*.2.	No. 87
A Dog lying down, head on paws.	Imp.		No. 91
A Hound lying down, head raised. (gl.)	Imp.		No. 93
A Dog lying down, head raised.	Imp.		No. 94
A Dog standing watching a Mouse. (gl.)	Imp.	*Cl*.1.	No. 89
A Sheep sitting down. (gl.)	Imp.	*Cl*.2.	No. 100
A Dog sitting, head raised. (gl.)	Imp.	*Cl*.1.	No. 101
*Boy and Girl (unclad) and kissing.	Imp.		No. 102
A Cat lying down, head raised. (gl.)	Unmk.	*Cl*.2.	No. 104
*A Rabbit crouching. (gl.)	Imp.	*Cl*.2.	No. 106
A Sheep sitting down, ⎫ (A pair, A Ram sitting down. ⎭ both gl.)	Imp.	*Cl*.1.	No. 108
*A Lamb. (gl.)	Unmk.	*Cl*.1.	No. 109
A Crouching Hare. (gl.)	Imp.	*Cl*.2.	No. 110
"Paysan Basque environs de Bayonne".	Imp.		No. 114
"Paysanne Basque des environs de Bayonne".	Imp.		No. 115
*Girl with a basket of flowers. (gl.)	Imp.	*Cl*.2.	No. 119
"Paysanne de St. Angelo". (gl.)	Imp.		No. 120
Bust of Lord Brougham.	Imp.		No mould number.
Bust of Mr. Wordsworth.	Imp.		No mould number.
Bust of Mr. Scott.	Imp.		No mould number.

Gl. means glazed, usually coloured or gilt, sometimes both.

Imp. means impressed.

Bisc. means the biscuit state. Except where specifically stated the models are in biscuit, though the glazed equivalent should turn up some day. Most of the glazed models are also known in the biscuit state. The busts seem to have no mould numbers.

The Imp. i.e. impressed marks are either: Griffin; "Rockingham Works, Brameld", or just, "Rockingham Works, Brameld", dependent on the space available. The very small pieces have no room for the impressed mark at all. They carry only the mould number and usually the gilder's mark—*C1*.

Subsequent to the compilation of this list Mr. G. R. P. Llewellyn kindly notified us of certain additional figures in Mrs. Llewellyn's collection which could well take their place in the series. The most important are: a pair of figures of a dog watching a mouse, the unmarked glazed piece is No. 98, the marked, biscuit model, No. 89 (this is the correct number); a small figure, 2⅝ in. high, dressed in white with a red cloak, griffin impressed and glazed, but without a mould number; a crouching rabbit or hare No. 78? (the 7 is very indistinct); a pair of pastoral figures, a girl seated feeding a sheep is marked and impressed No. 14, the male figure who plays a wind instrument and is accompanied by a dog is unmarked, both are glazed. (We have printed this information substantially in the form we have received it, both from Mr. Dawnay and Mr. Llewellyn).

Who was responsible for the modelling of these excellent Rockingham figures? The records we have studied give no indication. William Ely is reputed to have modelled the Fitzwilliam bust, presumably he also executed the other busts mentioned in the list. But was he the chief figure modeller? It seems unlikely. We can, however, make some speculations. The theatrical figures and the "Canton girls" afford a few clues. According to Haslem ([1]) and Dr. F. B. Gilhespy ([2]), Samuel Keys, a modeller at the Derby factory, made for that concern the figures of Liston as "Paul Pry" (mould No. 144 on the Derby list), Madame Vestris and other theatrical pieces. Edward Keys, also of Derby, was the modeller of a "Set of Tyrolese Minstrels" and "Canton girls", and also of several animal studies. Did the workmen who left Derby in 1826 bring to Swinton examples of the work of Samuel and Edward Keys which a Rockingham modeller, or modellers, faithfully reproduced? Or is the connection more direct?

[1] John Haslem. "The Old Derby China Factory Workmen and their Productions", 1876.

[2] Dr. F. B. Gilhespy. "Crown Derby Porcelain", 1951, and "Derby Porcelain", 1961.

N.B.—About twenty of the marked figures mentioned in this section may be seen in the Yorkshire Museum, by far the largest public collection.

Edward Keys is recorded as having left Derby in 1826. It could well be that he came to Rockingham and applied his skills for the next few years for the rejuvenated Brameld brothers. This would certainly meet the case for the "Canton girls", the "Tyrolean" figures and many of the animal models. The theatrical pieces could have been a special commission given to Samuel Keys whilst he was still a Derby workman (he is recorded as leaving the factory in 1830). Alternatively the two Keys might have come to a financial arrangement that their figures could be produced at Swinton under the supervision of a third party.

These are speculations and not facts. A great deal of careful and detailed research is needed before such hypotheses can be substantiated or disproved. Whether Edward Keys came to Rockingham in 1826 and became their chief modeller, or not, there can be no doubt of the close similarity of certain Derby and Rockingham figures. Unfortunately this similarity has produced complications. Many unmarked figures have been wrongly ascribed to Rockingham; their true origin being Derby (The models of Mr. Pickwick and Queen Victoria are cases in point). This incorrect attribution is particularly apparent with certain pastoral groups set upon a rococo base; many of these are the work of John Whitaker who modelled at Derby between 1830 and 1847. In the marked Rockingham series none of the figures has a rococo or scroll-work base (Plate VIIa).

The Rockingham figures are really finely modelled. The lines are clean and clear-cut, the workmanship delicate and precise. The glazed and coloured pieces may not be of the standard of the great eighteenth century potteries, but they are infinitely superior to the cheap Staffordshire china figures produced at any time in the last hundred years (and still being made today) which are so often called Rockingham simply because they happen to be ornamented with fine china threads. Why this particular detail has been seized upon as a Rockingham characteristic is hard to understand. One of the outstanding features of the marked animal models is the nature of their fur or fleece. In no single case is use made of fine china threads for this purpose. All the marked animals we have seen, and which are noted in the list have *smooth* coats. This is significant when one remembers that the basis for attribution of many unmarked figures is fleece and fur modelled in fine china threads.

It should be possible at some time in the future to complete the check-list of marked Rockingham figures. The authors would greatly appreciate the assistance of anyone who could reliably authenticate a figure not included in the present list.

The mark on models in this series is usually impressed into the body of the ware. "ROCKINGHAM WORKS BRAMELD" is the usual style, though pieces with the griffin (also impressed) are not unknown. Jewitt also mentions the addition of the word "ROYAL" to the title, an indication

121

that the figures were still being produced after 1830. Very few such pieces are on record, and we know of no pieces marked with a coloured stamp—"Manufacturer to the King", whereas several pieces bear the earlier red griffin mark, either alone or in addition to the impressed mark. Thus it seems reasonable to assume that the majority of these figures were made between 1826 and 1830. The round, or sometimes square, base of the figures usually has a circular piece about an inch in diameter, and a quarter of an inch deep, cut out from the centre. The red griffin mark has been found stamped in this indentation. The incised mould or series number is also to be found under the base of the figure. If there is no griffin mark the presence of these incised numbers is a useful aid to identification, although it must be added that the Derby factory also placed similar numbers under the base of many of their figures.

Outside this main series, two further groups of Rockingham figures merit attention. Several fine busts of Earl Fitzwilliam were modelled in biscuit ware; one in Rotherham Museum has the plinth decorated with a purple ground and a gilt grape-and-vine design (Plate VIb). Similar busts are to be found in the Sheffield and York museums, though with plain plinths. William Eley is reputed to have been the modeller. The York copy is inscribed, "William Wentworth Fitzwilliam, Earl Fitzwilliam, &c., &c., &c. Born May 30 1748. Died Feb. 8 1833". A number of unmarked busts of prominent personalities are also attributed to Rockingham. These include William IV, George IV, Cobbett, Wellington and Charles James Fox, the latter probably a representation based on the Nolleken's bust, placed in the Rockingham Mausoleum on the Wentworth estate. In Rotherham Museum are three magnificent scent jars also in biscuit ware, with applied floral decoration, each with a stopper in the same form. Though these are unmarked, they are recorded by Jewitt as having been at Wentworth House when he visited.

The second group of figures outside the main series is of great interest and rarity. Only a few models are known of these flat or backless figures and all are excellently modelled and delicately painted. From the front they appear to be the normal three-dimensional figure; closer inspection reveals that while the front is decorated, the back is concave and quite plain. Although the figure part is backless, the base or plinth is complete and rounded. We have only seen a few figures of this type—typical subjects are "The Boxers", "Chasseur aux Chamoix", "Don Quixote", "Sancho Panza". The latter piece is in the Rotherham collection, "The Boxers" in York. "Don Quixote" and "Sancho Panza" have the name in gilt in an oblong frame on the plinth of the figure; the lettering on the Chasseur is in black. It is possible that other figures or groups were modelled, and doubtless private collectors will know of such pieces. There is no impressed mould number; the printed griffin mark is used. "The Boxers" also bears the gilder's mark, *C1*.1. (See Appendix, note d, p. 141 below).

It is worth emphasising that the modelling of all the figures in the three groups just described is extremely fine. The decoration too, is careful and colourful. These figures stand in favourable comparison with the work of any of the Bramelds' contemporaries.

Turning to the unmarked figures the same difficulties are encountered that we have noted in connection with cottages and castles. Four main groups of unmarked figures have in the past been ascribed to Rockingham. The first group contains mainly of large figures quite well-modelled and decorated, but unmarked. These figures are clearly in a different style to the main marked series; in general they are not so precisely modelled or as carefully decorated as the pieces already described. The chief point of identification is the underside of the base. This recesses considerably and has a small circular hole in the centre— quite different from the marked models. Frequently such pieces have a gold line running round the base between ¼-in. and ½-in. from the foot. Examples of such figures can be seen in the public collections. The Victoria and Albert has a pair of Oriental figures over 12-in. high, in gaily coloured robes. York Museum has a sailor in a blue and white striped jersey, and Rotherham has a lively midshipman, and three negroes in dancing attitudes. All these, and a good number more of a similar type and standard of modelling, have been ascribed to Rockingham for many years. But one is bound to ask; if they were made at Swinton, why did the Bramelds fail to mark them? We can only pose the question, we cannot provide a definite answer. We believe, however, that before too long, careful research, now in progress in various quarters, will result in authoritative information being available upon which more reliable attributions can be based.

The figures in the second and third categories of unmarked pieces present greater problems. In the second group the indentation and hole in the base are present, and usually the gold line around the plinth. The third type of figure is hollow, and is said to have given service as a candle snuffer. Both these types of figure are crude, and often badly modelled; the quality of the porcelain is inferior, and they are generally smaller—between 2-in. and 4-in. is the normal height. They are at a long remove from the detailed perfection of the biscuit figures, or of "Lubin Log". This considerable stylistic gulf has led some authorities to question the attribution of these pieces. It is argued that the models are comparatively so crude that they could not have been produced by the same artists and modellers responsible for the marked series. As similar crude models were made at scores of Staffordshire potteries throughout the nineteenth century, it is impossible to separate the alleged work of the Bramelds from all the rest without one single marked piece to work upon. Certainly such an argument has stylistic and artistic evidence to support it.

The figures rejected by those who subscribe to these views are mainly peasant and pastoral groups. Men and women are depicted holding sheep, or standing with these and other animal (in many cases identification is based upon the modelling of the animals, and the use of the fine china threads discussed elsewhere). Simply dressed peasants sit upon barrels or in chairs quaffing ale. Sportsmen load their guns, or stand leaning upon the weapons admiring their dogs. Seated cross-legged turbaned gentlemen smoke hookahs. The full list of attributed models is extensive. The decoration of these pieces is coarser, the colours more garish than on the marked models.

The major galleries and most of the important private collections have plenty of examples of these two types of figures. Curators and collectors have for many years ascribed them without too much hesitation to Rockingham. Furthermore it should be already apparent that the Bramelds were usually ready to try "a new line". It is quite consistent with the "Brameld psychology" that in later years, the years of declining fortune, moulds should be fashioned and figures fired well below the standards of the "Royal" days. A new mass market might be captured with cheap, simple, colourful little china figures. Nor is it inconsistent with the known character of Thomas Brameld that he should put these wares upon the market unmarked. Crude figures stamped with his name would lower his reputation as a fine potter, a "Manufacturer to the King". These are only speculations, not facts. The facts are that these figures are unmarked, crudely modelled, fired from inferior materials and bear no resemblance to the signed pieces.

In our view these cheaper figures were not made at Swinton, their origin is Staffordshire, and sometimes a recent one. Nevertheless a few, though not the hundreds attributed, could be genuine Rockingham. The difficulty is to draw the line between the spurious and the possibly authentic. The difficulty has arisen from the paucity of documentary information on the Pottery's output and from the propensity of non-specialists to affix a respectable and "high class" name such as Rockingham to inferior wares emanating from Staffordshire potteries. Literally hundreds of cheap china figures can be found with a "Rockingham" ticket affixed to them. This proliferation of attributions has been much assisted by the persistence of the myth that the vast majority of Rockingham ware is unmarked. We suspect that the truth of the matter is that a considerable proportion of Rockingham *was* marked. Much of the unmarked "Rockingham" is not genuine Rockingham. This is clearly the case with tablewares and we believe it to be true of ornamental wares and of figures.

Possibly, hidden away somewhere, are figures of these two types clearly marked with the Rockingham imprint. Until such pieces come to light we do not feel justified in going beyond the statement that certain types of pastoral, peasant and sporting figures have been given the generic name "Rockingham", a term which may give no indication of their true origin.

Finally, we turn to the figures of animals attributed to Rockingham. Animals were popular subjects with both public and potter throughout the nineteenth century. Several different species are said to have been modelled at Rockingham, but it is the poodles which gained most popularity, and at the same time commanded the highest prices. In some ways this is difficult to understand, for so far as we are aware there is no recorded case of a marked poodle. In fact it is quite possible that the Swinton factory has gained a high reputation for a product it never even made! The position is similar to that indicated in the case of cottages, and the coarser coloured figures. As there are no marked pieces for comparison how can a firm attribution be made? The answer again is that a particular class of wares was recognised as having a specific origin, and that origin (rightly or wrongly) was attributed to Rockingham. In this instance the features which distinguish "Rockingham" poodles from inferior products, have also been used to make attributions for other unmarked animal models.

The outstanding feature of those pieces ascribed to Rockingham is the manner in which the hair of the animal is reproduced. The coat of such a poodle is made up of literally thousands of minute china strips. Naturally, these very fine strands adhere together, sometimes in quite sizeable sections; but the individual slivers are still discernable, and the overall effect is noticeably superior to that achieved by other methods. Close examination of even very small models will reveal this characteristic. The poodles attributed to the Pottery are modelled in a variety of shapes and postures.

The lack of contemporary documentary evidence on the factory's output is a severe handicap in establishing the authenticity of "Rockingham" poodles. Many models which are styled "Rockingham" are clearly of much more recent origin than the 1830's; the discerning can soon distinguish them. Furthermore, contemporary potteries—Derby and Grainger-Lee—are known to have modelled such pieces. The major galleries and private collections contain few examples, and a number of experts flatly reject the suggestion that poodles were modelled at Swinton. Certainly all the marked animal models—of dogs other than poodles and of sheep for example—depict the subjects with a smooth coat. Moreover it is not irrelevant to note that almost fifty years ago an article by a collector of pottery and porcelain animals seems to have fostered the belief that the Rockingham Pottery produced a considerable variety of poodle models. It is in such a manner that an unidentified piece which "looks as though it might possibly be

125

Rockingham", becomes in the course of time "quite definitely Rockingham". As in former cases we believe that these doubts should be raised in the best interests of historical accuracy, and we are confident that current research and modern techniques of analysis will eventually produce conclusive evidence of the authenticity, or otherwise, of "Rockingham" poodles.

Of the remaining types of animal modelled at Rockingham we have already mentioned the smooth-coated sheep. In addition rabbits, dogs and cats were made, both in biscuit and glazed and coloured (marked examples are indicated in the list).

Most of the other animal attributions are based on the presence of the fine porcelain threads already discussed. On this basis models of lions, cats and a plethora of sheep have been ascribed to Rockingham. The merits of such attributions have already been examined.

* * * *

(h) Miscellaneous Items.

In this section a brief reference will be made to various objects some of which were not manufactured in any quantity, and others which have a somewhat lesser intrinsic merit or attraction.

The candlesticks made by the Bramelds are rather crudely fashioned. They have a red, blue, and sometimes green ground, with a white foliage design in low relief. Personally we find them unattractive, but some collectors wax enthusiastic. Hand candleholders were also made. These, with handles attached to very short candlesticks, are interesting, but have no distinguishing feature. Candelabra are also recorded, though we have never seen a clearly authentic example.

Jewitt records a china table made at Swinton, and Mr. W. Mason told us of a similar piece he had once possessed which was about 2-ft. 3-in. in height, and attractively painted with butterflies and flowers. Very few such pieces can have been made.

In an attempt to gain increased custom some very curious small items were fashioned. Those of which we have knowledge, include thimbles, collar-studs (painted with a fox's head), and small china slippers, uncoloured but with gilt outlines. Some of these slippers were, like those made in the brownware, designed as inkwells. A number of brooches enclosing a small picture have survived; subjects including a Jewish woman (possibly Rebecca), Jesus Christ, and oddly within so limited a compass, Wentworth Woodhouse. It is probable that these miniatures were the work of one of the Baguleys, or of artists in their employ, and were not painted until after 1842.

We have already referred to toy teasets and small china animals, but other miniature objects deserve mention. Watering cans barely an inch in height, tiny patch-boxes, and extremely small scent bottles, have

PLATE XV

a. Porcelain figure of a hound. Length 4½in. Ht. 2¼in. (Mark 48, *impressed*, the griffin is indecipherable, and No. 93, *incised*). *Private collection.*

b. Small box in hard-paste porcelain with green ground and floral painting. 4in. × 2in. Ht. 1½in.

c. Underside of box showing fake griffin mark in brown. *T. A. Lockett.*

PLATE XVI

a. Two-handled
porcelain loving cup
with enamel painting.
(Puce griffin mark).
*Mr. and Mrs. J. G.
Evans.*

b. Ornamental pen-
holder in the form of
a shoe. Length 5in.
(Red griffin mark and
Cl 1). *Mr. and Mrs.
A. A. Eaglestone.*

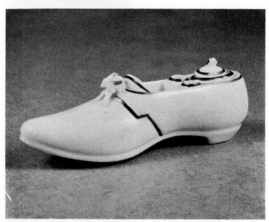

c. Small patch box.
Base in blue outlined
in gilt, coloured
encrusted flowers on
the lid. 3in. × 2¼in.
Ht. 1in. (Puce griffin
mark). *Mr. and Mrs.
F. N. Greaves.*

all been attributed to Rockingham. The scent bottles were usually decorated with coloured rosebuds and foliage applied in relief.

Scent bottles were in fact made in a variety of sizes, and sets of such vessels command good prices especially if marked and complete with stopper (Plate VIIIa). The applied flower decoration appears on many pieces, though others are painted with flowers or pastoral scenes. A number of finely modelled and decorated tobacco jars are said to have been made. A curious item (in the Sheffield Museum) is a dish in which stands an elephant supporting a castle having turrets into which pens or matches could be inserted. The piece is marked. One similar can also be seen in the Yorkshire Museum.

Decorative mugs with one or two handles must have been produced in some quantity; examples are known with fine flower and scenic painting and good gilding. The most interesting mugs are those bearing a portrait of the Duke of Wellington. One suspects that other celebrities were likewise portrayed, but Wellington seems to have been the only one to have survived. The mugs would probably appear in 1828 when the Duke became Prime Minister. The likeness, a faithful one, is taken probably from the Lawrence portrait. Several porcelain mugs have been noted with the horse's hoof-and-tail handle described earlier.

As we have already stated, in the late 1830's the Bramelds attempted to break into a new market by manufacturing bedposts, curtain rails and window heads. The design and decoration of these pieces is as pleasant as one could expect from such cumbersome articles. A curtain pole about six feet long, in sections, with a fluted centre piece may be seen in the Yorkshire Museum. In apple-green and white, it is marked with the griffin and Rockingham name, and bears the words "Dale's Patent" in acknowledgment of the inventor. Other such pillars, posts and rails, were (according to Jewitt) manufactured in pink and white, and decorated with flower paintings.

Far more practical and decorative were the jug and bowl sets; some individual jugs and ewers being extremely interesting. In the Sheffield Museum is a jug which bears a painting of the Manchester-Sheffield coach, "The Wellington Post". This piece ascribed to 1825 is not marked. If it is a genuine Rockingham item it is of more than usual interest since it represents a departure from the normal form of decoration. Unlike many potters the Bramelds rarely depicted scenes from contemporary life.

In the Yorkshire Museum is a jug with cover about which there can be no doubt since the piece is marked. The elaborate handles are in the form of a griffin, and a perforated container which fits inside the main piece has the words "Hobbs patent No. 26829" upon it. (Whether this container formed part of the original it is difficult to tell). The main jug, decorated in green and gold, and inscribed "LEECHES", could well have been part of a surgeon's equipment. Other jug and bowl sets are decorated more conventionally with flower groups, butterfly studies, rurai scenes and country mansions (Plate VIIc).

* * * *

It is unlikely that many hitherto unrecorded large trays or plaques will be discovered. We have already mentioned the Speight copy of the Vandyke Strafford picture, and views of Chatsworth and the Plains of Waterloo. Jewitt records a dish decorated with applied flowers and painted with a view of Arundel Castle, and Rotherham Museum has recently acquired the excellent fruit painting by Thomas Steel, illustrated in Plate IVb. Mrs. Llewellyn has in her collection a tray painted in the style of Randall with several exotic birds, and a slightly smaller tray of a seascape off the Isle of Wight. The artist is thought to have been Bailey, and the plate is marked on the back with the single word "Rockingham" in gilt. A pastoral scene and Wentworth House are also depicted on trays of similar size in the same collection. A few more may exist in the older country houses or in remote private collections, but the hopeful enthusiast is not likely to discover such a tray in the corner junk shop.

It is possible however, that a pen tray, or an ink-pot, or inkstand, could be found in this way. Flat pen trays are decorated in the usual style with views or floral designs, but the ink-pots and stands reveal a certain ingenuity of design and decoration. These range from the simple circular piece in the centre of which is the ink-well (Plate VIIIb), to extremely elaborate forms intended to stand upon large desks. An example of the latter type can be seen in the Sheffield Museum collection. Other unusual designs are worth noting. We have already pointed out the "Elephant and Castle" design, and china and brownware slippers adapted for the purpose. (The slippers are a copy of a French design). The fountain pen, and more recently the ball-point have made the inkstand as obsolete as the pastille burner, but a fine Rockingham piece which once graced an aristocratical desk or bureau, would certainly adorn a modern boardroom. A simple inkstand makes an attractive ornament for a home.

Finally, we must mention items of considerable rarity. Certain dessert services included ice-pails, which from time to time enter the market separate from the rest of the service. It is possible that a few of these pails were made to be sold independently. None of the major public galleries has such a pail, but a number are said to be in private hands. The decoration is of course, in the dessert service style. Rockingham snuff-boxes are rarely met with, probably because porcelain on account of its fragility did not lend itself to common use (John Wager Brameld presented a personally decorated one to Allen of Lowestoft). Liability to damage must have reduced greatly the number of small

128

model flowers. These fine items are generally in two parts, the whole being in fact a small container for scent, powder or some such cosmetic. A marked piece in excellent condition, of an open white rose with yellow stamens and five green leaves, was on display at a recent "Dealers Fair". Rotherham Museum has a rather damaged specimen which appears to represent an aster. This, coloured red, has also a spray of green leaves as its base. Aston is recorded as being the Pottery's flower modeller.

The artist Speight, is known to have painted at least one series of small decorative porcelain plaques. About 5-in. by 3-in. these are fine examples of technical accomplishment and artistry. Mr. M. E. Redfern has one such plaque in his collection. Edwin Steel would appear to have done similar work. A floral composition in Mrs. Llewellyn's collection bears all the signs of being his handiwork.

* * * *

It may well be that we have failed to mention certain items made by the Bramelds during the highest level of their achievement. Such omissions are inevitable when dealing with a lengthy term of sixteen years, and an establishment which for a great part of that time employed nearly six[1] hundred persons. Thomas Brameld was constantly casting around for new ideas, new designs, and new markets for his porcelain wares. The result of his industry was not only a multiplicity of patterns and designs, but an enormous range of items both useful and decorative. As time went on, and economic pressure bore heavily upon him, his standards tended to be modified. Decoration became less lavish, gilding less profuse. Despite this, when finally Thomas and his brethren were compelled to quit the Swinton Works, they were still producing many wares of the highest quality in a wide range of patterns and designs. The simpler wares may have reflected financial decline, but they were never cheapened artistically.

[1] This should read *three* hundred

5. SUMMARY.

These then, are some of the principal products made by the Bramelds in porcelain between 1826 and 1842. It should be remembered that throughout this period the earthenware and other pottery goods were still in production, and that except for the use of the mark ROCKINGHAM and similar variants, these pottery wares continued to be marked in exactly the same way as they were in the 1806-26 period. Thus in general it is not possible to make any certain statement about the date when the piece was made. (A full list of the marks can be found on pp. 132-134).

The collector of Rockingham porcelain may still find bargains if he is knowledgeable and diligent. The general increase in the value of antiques during the last few years is reflected in the prices asked for good Rockingham pieces. Information about prices is quickly out of date, and any prices we mention refer to 1963 unless otherwise stated. In April, 1954, a 127-piece dinner service, decorated with flower and butterfly paintings fetched nearly £1,000 at Christies. £330 was paid recently for a tea service; the highest price on record for a Rockingham service. Normally tea services of over twenty pieces can rarely be bought for under £2 a piece, and if the decoration is particularly good the price may be treble or even more. The larger vases and scent jars also tend to be expensive. An extremely fine and absolutely perfect set of three pot-pourri vases with covers, all marked, and each of a different size decorated with an abundance of applied flowers, was recently on offer for £300. The ordinary collector however, will be on the look-out for less expensive "buys". Single cups and saucers, with simple decoration can sometimes be bought for as little as five shillings each. Naturally, marked pieces fetch more, and a fine marked cup and saucer could well cost more than £12. The same is true of dinner and dessert plates. Three pounds can secure a good unmarked specimen which is simply decorated, but a marked plate finely painted might well be priced at £25 or even double. Other factors than marking and decoration enter into the computation of comparative prices. A long list of prices asked in antique shops, and paid at auction sales, could have been compiled, but this would have served only a limited purpose. London prices are vastly different from those asked in (say) a small Northern town. The large showroom will be many pounds up on the corner junk shop. And the level of prices in the Sheffield area is noticeably higher than that obtaining in areas further away from the site of the old works. We hope that the few examples cited will perhaps give a general indication of the present trend of prices. In fact, since this chapter was first written in 1962, prices have very nearly doubled for perfect pieces.

As some Rockingham pieces are unmarked, the collector with a *specialist* knowledge, while not armed at all points, has a distinct advantage. One sees in antique shops many examples of porcelain hopefully labelled "Rockingham" which superficially resemble the Swinton product. Closer examination of shape, paste, and decoration, show that it is not quite right. Such pieces as those decorated by the Baguleys using the Bramelds pattern book, especially wares with simple ground colours and gilding, are very close indeed. So, too, is the decorative work done at York by Hirstwood and his sons, all of them former Rockingham artists. John Wager Brameld's work after 1842 which was done in Bayswater, London, is in the same style, and there must be some pieces still in existence which were decorated by Robert Allen. In addition there are reproductions and downright fakes. Certain forgeries emanate from France, the rather crude reproduction of the griffin reveals them for what they are[1]. Obviously, even the expert cannot always be right in marginal cases, and frequently he will have to confess that he cannot be positive in his assessment.

Knowledge is perhaps the most important prerequisite in forming a collection—and a certain amount of money also. But without a knowledge of the paste, the decoration, the colours, the marks, and the style of the selected subject, money will only buy an assembly of doubtful specimens—unless, of course, one allows others to do the buying, in which case the real excitement of collecting is lost. Knowledge can be gained from books, visiting museums, talking to dealers, and other collectors, and from inspecting notable private collections. All approaches are valuable, but to look at, and wherever possible to handle as many pieces as one can, is the surest line. It is surprising how quickly, once one begins to feel that one has gained an understanding of the wares, order emerges from seeming chaos. Such an observation is true of anything one chooses to collect, but it has a particular relevance to Rockingham porcelain for reasons we have explained.

There are still plenty of opportunities to collect Rockingham, even though the would-be collector possesses only a slender purse. But time is running out. As the price of 18th century wares becomes prohibitive, many collectors turn perforce to the early 19th century, and even to the Victorian era. This is all to the good. We believe that the history of the Rockingham factory and its wares which have never before been fully considered, will receive far more attention during the next decade than they have done during the past fifty years. The Rockingham Pottery has for too long been underestimated, and we trust that this study will make amends for the neglect of the past.

[1] G. A. Godden's *British Pottery and Porcelain 1780-1850* contains interesting information on fakes and forgeries of Rockingham wares.

6. MARKS ON ROCKINGHAM POTTERY AND PORCELAIN

Earthenware

1.   This is the earliest recorded mark on earthenware. It is noted in the catalogue of the Boynton Collection, and in Jewitt, but we have been unable to trace a piece so marked. The mark would date from the period when Bingley was the chief proprietor (1778-85), or possibly from the period of the Leeds ownership (1785-1806) when Bingley was a partner. No other mark can be positively attributed to this early period.

2-10.   There are many variants of the Brameld marks for the period 1806-42. Marks 2-10 give the name Brameld followed by a number with a + sign between. There is no obvious meaning to these numbers, though they might indicate a date sequence. Probably their significance is limited to the internal organisation of the Pottery. All impressed.

11-20.   This group of marks has the name followed by a symbol. The marks are confined to various kinds of earthenware and brownware. All impressed.

21-25.   Tea, coffee, chocolate and "Cadogan" pots often bear one of the marks 2-20, but certain marks exclusive to these pots have been noted. They are shown as 21-25. All impressed.

26.   Cane coloured stoneware was invariably marked embossed in the colour of the relief decoration. The garland around the border of the cartouche consists of roses, shamrock and thistles. A similar mark, with no outer rim, is found impressed on earthenware items.

27-34.   *Stone* china usually bears an impressed Brameld mark, and in addition a more elaborate and decorative printed mark. Eight such marks are listed, 27-34.

35-37.   Certain earthenware items made after 1826 carry the word "Rockingham" in the mark. It is believed, however, that the customary "Brameld" marks continued to be used after 1826, side by side with "Rockingham" marks. The Rockingham marks are shown as 35-37. Apart from the teapot with MORTLOCK'S ROYAL ROCKINGHAM the inclusion of the word "ROYAL" has not been noted on any pottery or earthenware piece. All impressed.

Porcelain

38.   This mark, pencilled in red script, is noted in the Catalogue of the Boynton Collection. It is a very rare mark and was probably used only on trial pieces in the period 1820-26. We have not been able to locate a piece bearing this mark.

39.	This mark, in script, is on the base of a cup in the Rotherham Museum collection. It is the only known example, and was almost certainly used *before* the griffin stamp was ready for use.
40.	The normal mark found on porcelain in the period 1826-30. It is printed in red.
41.	A rarer mark from the 1826-30 period. The Rotherham copy of the "Rhinoceros" vase is marked in this way. Printed in red.
42-44.	These three marks, printed in puce, date from the period 1830-42, when the word "Royal" was added to the title of the Pottery. No. 42, "Manufacturer to the King", is the most commonly found of the three.
45.	A more elaborate mark from the 1830-42 period. This particular example is taken from the basket showing a view of Clifton Park plate VIa. The Royal Service pieces carry a similar mark, printed twice on some of the comports in puce.
46.	A cartouche or embossed mark similar to that found on stoneware jugs and mugs has been noted on certain items of porcelain ware. The mark is normally in blue, the colour of the relief decoration.
47.	A few wares of the highest quality, often enamelled with pictures bearing the artist's signature, carry this mark. It is written in gilt lettering on the back of the piece.
48-49.	Biscuit figures and the base of certain coloured figures bear the impressed mark (48). Much more rarely such pieces carry mark 49, either with or without the griffin. A number of figures have been noted bearing the red *printed* griffin mark. There are no recorded cases of a printed griffin from the "Royal"—post 1830—period on Rockingham figures.
50-52.	Llewellyn Jewitt records certain other marks. We have not encountered them in the form in which he expresses them.

Baguley Marks

| 53. | This mark presents certain problems. It is often quoted as a Brameld mark, used for a short period after 1837. It should be noted that the mark does not include the name Brameld. As far as we are aware the mark has only been recorded on brown glazed ware. Whilst it is possible that the Bramelds used this mark in sanguine expectation of Queen Victoria's patronage, there are strong reasons for believing that it is a mark used for a period by Isaac Baguley after he had taken over the Works. Supporting this belief is an interesting |

133

variant of the mark which occurs on a brown glazed saucer in our own collection. The mark, printed in red, has been placed *over* the anchor mark of *Samuel Barker and Son.* Barker of Mexborough acquired the Don Pottery in the late 1830's, but only began to trade under the name of Samuel Barker & *Son* in 1852, long after the Bramelds had ceased to manufacture. (See note c, below).

Why Baguley should claim to have been a "Manufacturer to the Queen" remains obscure, but the mark certainly seems to be his and not the Bramelds.

54-56.   Baguley's other recorded marks which appear on both china and earthenware are shown as 54, 55, 56.

57.   The mark used by *Alfred* Baguley after he transferred his business to Mexborough in 1865.

Notes—
a.   We have already stressed the importance of pattern numbers on table-ware items (p. 103). Where no other mark is found, the numbers can be a help with identification.

b.   Mention has also been made of the letters *C1*—followed by a number—which appear on certain decorative pieces. These markings are important for the purposes of identification as no other factory seems to have used such a notation (see p. 114).

c.   This attribution is incorrect. The anchor and the initials S.B. & Son is the mark of Sampson Bridgwood & Son of the Anchor Pottery, Longton. It is this concern and not Samuel Barker and Son which supplied the Baguleys with wares in the white.

MARKS ON ROCKINGHAM POTTERY AND PORCELAIN

Pottery

1 **BINGLEY**   2 **BRAMELD+1**   3 **BRAMELD+2**   4 **BRAMELD+4**

5 **BRAMELD+5**   6 **BRAMELD+6**   7 **BRAMELD+7**   8 **BRAMELD+10**

9 **BRAMELD+11**   10 **BRAMELD+12**   11 **BRAMELD**   12 **BRAMELD+**

13 **BRAMELD++**   14 **BRAMELD+ .**   15 **BRAMELD✚**   16 **BRAMELD ✷**

17 **BRAMELD * ***   18 **BRAMELD✚✚**   19 **BRAMELD & Co.**   20 **BRAMELD+△**

21 **MORTLOCK**   22 **CADOGAN**   23 MORTLOCK'S CADOGAN   24 **NORFOLK**

25 MORTLOCK'S ROYAL ROCKINGHAM

26

27

28

29

30

31   [A PARROQUET]
Parroquet Fine Stone B
(Printed in Blue)
BRAMELD+

32

KAOLIN
Griffin printed in
red. Kaolin im-
-pressed.

33   [A HAND]
BRAMELD+7

34   [A BIRD]
Genuine Opaque China
BRAMELD+7

35   ROCKINGHAM
BRAMELD

36   ROCKINGHAM

37   *Rockingham*

Porcelain

38   *Brameld*

39   Rockingham
China Works
Swinton 1826

40

41

42

43

44

45

46

48

47

49

ROYAL
ROCKINGHAM
WORKS
BRAMELD

50   [*GRIFFIN*]   **51**
ROYAL ROCKINGHAM
BRAMELD

[*GRIFFIN*]
ROYAL ROCKINGHAM
WORKS
BRAMELD

52

[*GRIFFIN*]
**BRAMELD
ROYAL
ROCKINGHAM
WORKS**

Baguley Marks

53

54

55

56   [*NO GRIFFIN*]
Baguley
Rockingham Works

57

7. ADDENDUM: RECENT RESEARCH AND DISCOVERY 1964-73

Since the first edition of this book was published, there has been much sound research and publication on the factory and its wares by keen Rockingham collectors. The chief publications are listed here: D. G. Rice, *Rockingham Ornamental Porcelain* (*R.O.P.*), The Adam Publishing Co., 1965, which deals in detail with the factory's ornamental porcelain, and, D. G. Rice, *Rockingham Pottery and Porcelain* (*R.P. & P.*), Barrie & Jenkins, 1971, a well-illustrated, full survey of the factory's output.

Articles: T. A. Lockett, *Collectors Guide*, January 1964, February and March 1965, and A. A. Eaglestone and T. A. Lockett, *The Connoisseur*, July 1966 (these four are all general articles); T. A. Lockett, "The Bramelds in London", *The Connoisseur,* June 1967; J. G. and M. I. N. Evans, *The Antique Collectors Club* magazine (*A.C.C.*), February, March, April and September, 1969 (the four articles admirably cover the range of the pottery's products); A. A. and E. M. Eaglestone, "Rockingham tewares", *Collectors Guide,* October 1969; Angela Cox and T. A. Lockett, "The Rockingham Pottery a preliminary excavation", *The Connoisseur,* March 1970; Alwyn and Angela Cox, "New light on large Rockingham vases", *The Connoisseur,* April 1970.

To the history of the factory as contained in Part I, little has been added. Further details of the activities of the Bramelds after the factory closure are contained in both of Dr. Rice's books and in our own article on "The Bramelds in London", but in substance the story set out on pp. 7-80 needs no amendment. On the Royal dessert service (p. 50), recently published research (T. A. Lockett, *Davenport Pottery & Porcelain 1794-1887*, David & Charles, 1972) has revealed that Davenport were competitors for William IV's favour. Examples of the Davenport service still exist and are reproduced in the quoted work. The Dyson Perrins Museum has a sample of the Worcester product, but no evidence of a Derby service has come to light, if indeed one was ever commissioned.

On p. 55 a list of patterns is given with the names of artists attached. Dr. Rice (*R.O.P.* p. 80) has correctly pointed out that Mr. Wilson and Mr. Child were customers and not artists. As to his speculation that we may have misread the names of Hoyland (Leyland), Ross (Rouse) and Russell (Randall), all we can add is that we have been unable to check this, as most regretably all further access to the pattern books has been denied to us and, we understand, to other students also.

Reference is made on p. 68 to the TWIGG dish printed with a view of the Pottery. We were privileged to see at Wentworth Wodehouse a BRAMELD marked dish with the same scene well printed in blue. Further examples would be outstanding collectors' items.

Turning to the wares, we find that though many additional shapes patterns and types of ware have come to notice, the general outline we advance on pp. 82-134 still stands, as do the speculations concerning figures, cottages and poodles. These we shall consider in detail later.

Of the earliest wares, those produced between 1745 and 1785, we still know nothing. Odd fragments of combed slipware and black, iron-glazed ware are to be found on the site, but not in archaeological context. In this connection, in the "dig" of 1967 at the lowest level shards of Leeds-type creamware were uncovered (illustrated in *The Connoisseur*, March 1970). These appeared to date from the period 1785-1806. Apart from these shards nothing additional is known of the wares of this period. A second excavation in 1968 aimed at uncovering fragments from this pre-Brameld period was unsuccessful. We can only re-iterate our speculation (p. 85) that the wares were unmarked or bore the impress of the Leeds Pottery.

For the Brameld period (1806-42) many interesting earthenware pieces have emerged in the past decade. In brown-glazed ware (pp. 86-92) certain revisions need to be made. We noted shoe warmers, furniture supports, frog mugs and candlesticks (p. 91) as items made in brown glazed earthenware. No marked pieces have been recorded, and thus it would be prudent to regard these items as not having been made at Swinton. On the other hand, marked examples of the snuff-taking squire (two sizes 9-in and 7-in high), milk jugs in a low "round Egyptian" shape, a teapot modelled as a tree trunk with rustic handle and spout, water jugs and broth bowls as well as the more familiar Cadogan pots (in three sizes $7\frac{1}{2}$-in, $6\frac{1}{2}$-in, and $4\frac{1}{2}$-in high), and tea and coffee pots, either in plain brown glaze or embellished with flowers or chinoiserie in gilt are all genuine products of the Bramelds.

By 1806 the heyday of cream-coloured earthenware had passed. Nevertheless, some marked Brameld items are known in addition to the botanical plates mentioned on p. 94. A dish finely enamelled with a bird is shown here (Plate IXa). The decoration would appear to be unique, though two similar dishes with scenic views are illustrated in G. A. Godden's, *Illustrated Encyclopaedia of British Pottery & Porcelain* (Plate 495). Additionally, a marked, plain, pierced plate is known, and a most remarkable and handsome jug was recently auctioned. The sides are decorated with oval cartouche containing painted cricketing scenes and beneath the lip is a view of a castle. The jug is $9\frac{1}{2}$-in high and is marked BRAMELD & Co. SWINTON POTTERY (See D. G. Rice, *R.P. & P.* Plate 38). Probably very little true creamware was made after 1810, in fact the statement on p. 92 which implies that underglaze transfer printing was done on creamware is a little misleading. It would perhaps be more accurate to regard the body for printing as either a pearlware or an ordinary earthenware one.

Since we first wrote on the printed wares (pp. 92-3) very considerable interest has been generated in this class of ware. As we paid only passing attention to it in 1964, we accord it fuller treatment here and include an additional five illustrations of printed pieces. Of these, the "Apple gatherers" (Plate XIIa) and the "Floral Sketches" pattern have never been illustrated before, and the "Three urns" (or "Dustbin"!) pattern (Plate XIIc) is normally only found on porcelain. The Willow pattern (Plate IXb) is seen here in conjunction with two unusually-shaped pieces, the heart-shaped side dish and the hot-water plate. Brameld Willow pattern is not particularly abundant. The baskets (Plate XIa and b) are unusual in form. Such shapes have not been illustrated before.

The following are the currently-recorded *underglaze blue* printed patterns: *Don Quixote* (Plate Ib, a dozen different scenes were used on different pieces of a service); *the Woodman* (Plate Ib); *Castle of Rochefort: South of France* (Plate IIb); *Twisted tree* (Plate IIb): *Willow* (Plate IXb); *Sweet peas* (Plate XIb); *the Apple gatherers* (Plate XIIa); *the Three Urns* (Plate XIIc); *Floral sketches* (Plate XIIIa). The patterns *Parroquet* and *Flower groups* are illustrated by Dr. Rice (*R.P. & P.*) and by the Evans who additionally show *The Llandeg blackberry border* (*A.C.C.* March and April 1969). *The Forfarshire* with the *Floral Border* (*The Connoisseur*, July 1966); *Indian flowers* (unpublished, in Rotherham Museum); *Burns cottage* (unpublished, Sheffield Museum): *Paris stripe* (unpublished); *Bo-peep* (*The Connoisseur*, March 1970); *Boy Fishing* (*The Connoisseur*, March 1970) *Swinton Pottery* (unpublished, but as in the frontispiece). Additionally, a pattern of stylised flowers appears *painted* underglaze on some wares. Some of the above patterns were also printed in black or green, with or without enamel colours and gilding. Certain patterns appear only in colours other than blue. We have already noted (p. 93) the hunting scene and *For Sarah;* also recorded are *For Martha—what pretty toys* and *For Samuel.* Mr. and Mrs. Evans also illustrate (*A.C.C.*, March 1969) a multi-coloured plate with a basic print of a Greek key border and an exotic bird and foliage; also a composite country-and-town scene printed in black. If we add to these a rare over-coloured chinoiserie "girl at the window" print (Evans, *A.C.C.* April 1969) and the green flower print found in association with the rare earthenware teaware set (Eaglestone, *Collectors Guide*, October 1969) the number of printed patterns considerable exceeds our earlier anticipation. Undoubtedly more will be discovered, particularly variants of floral motifs.

One further printed pattern should be mentioned, this is the unique coloured Imari-type pattern (Plate XIIb). This is very reminiscent of the designs appearing on Masons Patent Ironstone and Davenport and Spode stone china. But the Bramelds never made a true stone china of the hard, durable, grey-tinted body such as the Staffordshire firms produced. Brameld used the terms "granite china", and "fine stone" but the ware has none of the toughness of their competitors (See p. 93).

In cane coloured stoneware (p. 93), in addition to the jugs and mugs we noted, a fine covered jug moulded with daisy heads on the upper portion; several shaped dishes with sprigged decoration and, most interesting of all, a tea service sprigged with classical rustic scenes in blue, have all been recorded (Rice, *R.P. & P.*, Plate 45).

On p. 94 we commented upon the rarity and fragility of the green glazed plates. Two of the four known shapes are illustrated here (Plate Ia) but two additional rarities were discovered by Mr. Gwyn Evans, the lotus vase (in the V. & A.), and the Keep of Conisboro' Castle. Both are unmarked so their attribution cannot be positive, but as Mr. Evans rightly remarks, "the potting and the quality of the glaze is of a high order and consistent with the attribution to Swinton". (Evans, *A.C.C.*, February 1969). A jug with daisy-head moulding and a Cadogan in green glaze have also been reported.

Two other types of ware demand special mention. Yellow-glazed ware is exceedingly rare (no fragments were unearthed in the excavation) but two jugs—one with cover—moulded as pineapple are in the Leon collection at the Smithsonian Institution, Washington. They were first illustrated and described in the *Transactions of the English Ceramic Circle*, 1971 (p. 35, Plate 41c). Secondly, black basalts: Plate Xa shows fragments excavated on the site in 1967, the matching teapot in Xc was reported as a result of the publication of our finds. Still no marked pieces are recorded other than the small plaque illustrated in H. M. Grant, *The Makers of Black Basalts* (Plate LXXXIX). The fragments shown here in Plate Xb may assist further identification of unmarked pieces.

Finally on earthenware, we may note the plate marked "BRAMELD & BECKITT" with the date 1842 and the battle honours, CABOOL, LASWAREE and FREAZIPOOR of the 33rd Bengal Native Infantry. (Plate XIId). Though not of Brameld manufacture it is a reminder of the continuing association with the pottery trade by members of the family after manufacture had ceased at the Swinton works. (See *The Connoisseur*, June 1967.)

Although we personally find the study of the earthenwares fascinating, the generality of collectors are more attracted to the splendour of the porcelain, and much detailed work has recently been done on four main aspects of porcelain production; on tea wares, dessert and dinner wares, figures and the ornamental wares. Concerning tea wares, the pattern range we give on p. 103 has been extended slightly. It should now read 407-1563 with the second series 2/1 to 2/100 with an isolated piece recorded as high as 2/143. We can also be more precise about shapes. Plate XIVb shows the four most common cup shapes. The top left piece has an angular handle with a scallop edge and fluted sides to the ware, it is an early form from the red griffin period and the handle form is common to at least Davenport and Coalport, though in the Rockingham piece the handle does not protrude over the top of the cup rim. The cup on the bottom left is also of the red griffin period, the pieces are circular in form and the handle shape is roughly that of a figure 7. The top right cup has a handle of rustic or crabstock form and is associated with basket-weave moulding on the pieces. The fourth cup has the characteristic three-spur handle of the neo-rococo, post-1830 period and the teapot and sucrier in services of this form have the crown finial. Four other handle forms deserve mention, the crossed rustic which is associated with primrose leaf moulding, a single spur rustic, a single spur plain and the horse's hoof handle—this latter is found in association with Empire-style pieces with a teapot spout of phoenix form. There are other handle forms but the eight listed are by far the most common. Further details and fuller illustrations can be found in Evans, *A.C.C.*, April 1969 and Eaglestone, *Collectors Guide*, October 1969. Two factors need stressing, although pattern numbers appear on most pieces—except covers—the griffin mark will only be found on saucers, furthermore some services have been found with small cup plates of various sizes and others with "twiflers", small 7-in side plates (see p. 107).

Dessert and dinner service pattern numbers (p. 103) also require modification. The present known range is 416 to 875. We illustrate (Plate XIIIb) an octagonal dessert plate with the highly characteristic shell and gadroon edge of the early red griffin period. Another dessert plate shape from this period is circular with less-pronounced gadrooning and eight moulded anthemia on the rim. When a plate is unmarked the moulding is by far the best means of assessing whether it is Rockingham or not. Also illustrated are the primrose leaf moulding (Plate IIIb); the "royal" shape (Plate IIIa) formed with shark's teeth and four sets of "S" scroll moulding (a rarer variant is circular with shark's teeth and four sets of acanthus leaf and shell mouldings); Plate Vb shows the wavy edged plate with raised moulded "C" scrolls— the most common shape in the puce griffin period. Three further shapes are occasionally met with, an octagonal plate with famille verte decoration (see p. 111); a twelve-sided plate with gadroon edge and four sets of acanthus leaf and shell moulding, and finally the hitherto unrecorded wavy-edged hexagonal shape depicted in Plate XIIIc. Other shapes have been noted but only in single specimens. The shapes of other pieces in a service in general match the plates, for example, the fine tureen stand (Plate XIVa) though unmarked can unhesitatingly be assigned to Rockingham on account of the handle forms and the raised "C" scroll moulding which place it as belonging to a service of that plate form.

Turning to the ornamental items (pp. 112-116), the outline we provide has stood the test of time quite well. Much greater precision has been brought to the task of authentication by the publications of Geoffrey Godden on Minton and Coalport and Leonard Whiter in his book on Spode. Additionally, Dr. Rice has made a detailed study of this aspect of Rockingham production and the reader is referred to his specialist work for a systematic treatment of the types of vases and baskets made at the factory.

On cottages and castles (p. 116-7) our speculations have been amply justified. Even the antique trade is reluctantly abandoning the universal ascription "Rockingham cottage". Curiously enough, just one isolated item has appeared in this category. It is a flat backed piece which forms the right hand side of a thatched-roof cottage. A bush is prominent to the right hand of the piece out of which appears a cat its eyes intent upon a pair of doves perched above an open sash-window. The piece is coloured and bears a genuine griffin mark. It would seem to be the side piece of one of the three-part cottages which are met with occasionally. At all events it is an isolated oddity, which does not shake the general thesis that the factory was not responsible for the plenitude of cottages and castles formerly attributed to it.

On figures we advanced the proposition that the wise collector would do well to confine his attentions to the range of figures we indicated in the list (p. 118-9). This judgment and Major G. N. Dawnay's original theories have been fully confirmed. No figures of the type discussed on pp. 123-126 can be regarded as of Rockingham origin, nor can the fleecy poodles and sheep—they never saw Swinton. Fully marked examples of the type have been recovered from the factory site of Samuel Alcock of the Hill Top Pottery Burslem.

Since the 1964 list was compiled a number of additional figures have been recorded, these are noted below.

DESCRIPTION	TYPE OF MARK	GILDER'S MARK	MOULD NUMBER
Peasant girl with milk pail.	Red, printed		No. 2
John Liston as "Billy Lackaday"	Red, printed		No. 8
John Liston as "Moll Flaggon" (gl.)	Red, printed		No. 10
"Paysanne de Schlier en Tirol"	Imp.		No. 14
Bacchus (gl.)	Imp.		No. 32
Boy holding a dog ⎱ A pair Girl holding a sheep ⎰	Imp.		No. 35
"Chef du Tartares Noguars"	Imp.		No. 49
An elephant (gl.)	Unmk.	Cl.2.	No. 69
Hound lying down head raised (gl.)	Imp.		No. 92
Hound running (gl.)	Imp.		No. 93
A swan (gl.)	Unmk.	Cl.2.	No. 99
A cat and three kittens (gl.)	Imp.		No. 107

A squirrel (gl.)	Unmk.	*Cl.2.*	No. 111
"Homme de peuple à Valence (gl.)	Imp.		No. 113
A peacock (gl.)	Imp.		No. 136

In addition it should be noted that in No. 22 the word is Sagran; No. 65 would seem to be a misreading for 63 and should be deleted; No. 93 is incorrectly described in our original list, it is in fact a hound running as can be seen from Plate XVa where it is illustrated for the first time; No. 119 is entitled "Femme de L'Andalousie". Certain un-numbered figures are recorded including "Tristram Sappy", two separate figures of a pug dog and a pug bitch, and a cat on an oval base. Two further biscuit bust figures are now known, of George IV and the Duke of York—the latter in two sizes.

As pendant to the above it is worth recording some interesting information concerning the theatrical figures kindly sent to us by Mr. Anthony Oliver. He notes that John Liston appeared in "Lubin Log's Journey to London", first produced at the Coburn in 1820. Simon Pengander (Plate VIIa) was a character in Poole's "Twixt the Cup and the Lip" which opened at the second Haymarket Theatre on 12 June 1826. Even more significant is a print by J. H. Lynch (in the Enthoven collection) of Liston as Pengander exactly as he appears in the Rockingham figure. Clearly the modeller of the theatrical figures—probably Samuel Keys—worked from the published prints of both Liston and Vestris who were at the height of their fame in the 1820s.

In the miscellaneous section pp. 126-129 we note a variety of wares in the ornamental category. Here again careful research by Dr. Rice, Mr. and Mrs. Evans and others has greatly added to the scope of our knowledge of the factory's output. The reader is again referred to their published work for further examples. Special mention should be made of the discovery of the famous "Dragon" vases (p. 112) by Dr. and Mrs. Cox. Their admirable article on these pieces and the additional material they provide on the rhinoceros vases is well worth attention (*The Connoisseur*, April 1970). We illustrate here a finely decorated loving cup (Plate XVIa); a curious pen holder in the form of a shoe (Plate XVIb) and a tiny patch box (Plate XVIc) which may stand as representatives of a very wide range of miscellaneous items both useful and decorative.

Finally, in the section on marks, we may note that certain variants of the printed marks (marks 27-34) have been noted which correspond with the new printed patterns mentioned earlier (e.g. *Paris Stripe*, and *Floral Sketches, Granite China*). A curious impressed mark FIRE-PROOF/BRAMELD/DEEP MINE/IMPROVED was a product of the excavation, but none of the stone-coloured kitchen wares to correspond have yet been reported. The marks 50-52 which we had not seen have occurred, as have further variants of the BRAMELD +

with a variety of dots and stars. Dr. Rice advances a theory (*R.P. & P.* p. 102-3) that earthenware marked BRAMELD was predominantly pre-1826, and that impressed ROCKINGHAM predominantly post-1826. The latter part of this statement is probably accurate, but the former implies the discontinuation of transfer printed ware and other BRAMELD marked types seems wide of the mark. The excavation unearthed porcelain and earthenware in a layered context from the early 1830s, moreover, the shapes of the Don Quixote wares in particular with the "C" scroll and foliate edges so match the porcelain of the post-1830 neo-rococo period that they must surely be the "new shapes . . . of improved earthenware" of which John Wager Brameld writes in 1832. (see p. 62). All the evidence we have points to the continuation of earthenware production during the 1830s and to the continued use of the impressed BRAMELD mark.

Our last illustration (Plate XVa and b) is an example of a fake Rockingham piece and mark. This hard paste fake is well potted and nicely decorated, it seems to be of 19th century Continental manufacture possibly by Samson of Paris. Fortunately, the number of such fakes is few, and the shape and style of this particular example would not deceive the collector who knew his Rockingham, but its existence is salutary.

In our previous final summary (p. 130-31) we wrote of the specialist knowledge needed by the enthusiast. We have been gratified to see so much additional research undertaken since this book was first published in 1964. Anyone starting to study Rockingham in 1973 has a comparative wealth of research literature to assist him, in marked contrast to our own position over a decade ago. We are grateful to our publishers for the opportunity of making available again this first book on the Rockingham Pottery, and for incorporating the additional illustrations and textual comment.

8. SOURCES

Llewellyn Jewitt. *The Ceramic Art of Great Britain.* (1st Edit. 1878).

Oxley Grabham. *Yorkshire Potteries, Pots and Potters.* From the Annual Report of the Yorkshire Philosophical Society (1915).

A. Hurst. *Catalogue of the Boynton Collection of Yorkshire Pottery* (1922).

The Victoria County History of Yorkshire Vol. 2.

The Fitzwilliam (Wentworth) Papers—Sheffield City Library.

The Rotherham Borough Library "Rockingham Files", containing a number of items of interest.

H. G. Brameld. *Rockingham China and Its Makers.* (1910)—basically a condensed version of Jewitt.

Articles in *The Connoisseur*, notably an important article on marks by Mr. G. R. P. Llewellyn in the *Connoisseur Year Book, 1962.*

W. B. Honey. *English Pottery and Porcelain* (5th Edit. 1962).

G. A. Godden. *British Pottery and Porcelain 1780-1850.* (1963).

G. A. Godden. *Victorian Porcelain* (1961).

D. Towner. *The Leeds Pottery* (1963).

F. A. Barrett. *Caughley and Coalport Porcelain.* (1955).

John Guest. *Historic Notices of Rotherham* (1879).

Ebenezer Rhodes. *Excursions in Yorkshire* (1826).

In the Victoria and Albert Museum is a small manuscript pocket book used by Thomas Brameld c.1806-13, the principal contents being recipes for bodies and glazes with the potter's comments thereon. Ref.: MS. Brameld & Co. 463/1905 in the Manuscript Collection. A photocopy is in the Rotherham Public Library.

Note—

Llewellyn Jewitt, F.S.A., was born 24th November, 1816, at Kimberworth, near Rotherham.

A prolific writer and artist, he contributed to many popular journals. In 1866 he founded and edited *The Reliquary*, a Quarterly Archaeological Journal and Review. He was a contributor for many years to the *Art Journal* (his first notice of the Rockingham Pottery appeared in its pages in 1865).

He made pottery one of his special interests. His best known work being *"The Ceramic Art of Great Britain*, from Prehistoric times down to the Present Day, being a History of the Ancient and Modern Pottery and Porcelain Works of the Kingdom, and of their Productions of every Class".

Jewitt's *Ceramic Art* has been, since its first publication in 1878, the source book for pottery and porcelain commentators of all kinds, certain writers copying from the copyists.

Born at Kimberworth, he had a special interest in South Yorkshire where he made local enquiries, talking to those who remembered the Rockingham and Don Potteries in action.

Thus, Jewitt's book is a work of great importance. He worked conscientiously with the material he found to hand. What he did not, and in the circumstances could not, use, were the letters and other documents now available in the Wentworth Papers. Thus some of his observations on the Swinton Pottery, particularly concerning production and finance, need in the light of later research, to be adjusted.

APPENDIX

**Sale of China, Earthenware, Biscuit ware and other Effects at the
Rockingham Pottery, Swinton, May 1st, 2nd and 4th, 1843.**

Since the main body of the book was printed we have been able
to discover details of the sale of the Pottery effects, referred to on
pp. 73 and 74. The auction sale was conducted by Mr. Edward Lancaster
of Lancaster & Sons, Barnsley. The Firm still exists, and preserved with
the records is the Auction Book for 1843. We are grateful to Mr. A. W.
Lazenby, F.A.I. and Mr. G. L. Stirling, F.A.I. two of the Principals of
Lancaster & Sons for allowing us to consult this book, and for supplying
additional information.

The sale was a large one, and, judging by the number of different
purchasers, well attended. Prominent among the buyers were a Mr.
Holasworth and a Mr. Ogelsby—of whom we have no record. The more
familiar names of Barker, and Bagley (*Baguley*) also appear several
times, as does Copeland (purchasing tureens, chamber services and
china jugs).

The wares sold were principally table wares, as the sale announcement indicated. A few items selected more or less at random are printed
below. It must be remembered that many would be undecorated wares
commanding a lower price than finished pieces; furthermore price
values have greatly changed in the last 120 years. The pound in terms
of 1964 values should be multiplied by 8 or even 10.

	£	s.	d.
Doz. White China cups and saucers		2	6
3 doz. Mugs		3	0
72 Breakfast cups and saucers		4	6
24 Sugar bowls		2	0
2 Scent jars	2	16	0
2 Biscuit figures		3	6
2 Match pots		4	0
Cadogan teapot		6	6
Pair ornamental figures		4	6
Painted dish tray	1	12	0
China dessert service (burnished)	3	6	0
Burnished China tea service	2	0	0
2 China vases	4	8	0
Pair of fruit baskets		18	0
Bust		5	0
Asparagus dish		3	0
Chamber service		4	0
12 Drainers		1	0

	£	s.	d.
115 piece dinner service	2	12	0
3 doz. mustards		2	9
6 Wine coolers		1	6
24 China pen trays		5	0
Sundry honey pots		1	6
2 China bowls	1	0	0

The total amount realised at the sale was, China and Earthenware, £198 1s. 1d. (including certain pieces sold to Mr. Baguley by private contract). Furniture, £31 7s. 3d. (of which the pianoforte accounted for £8 15s. 0d.) and Farm implements, £8 3s. 9d. A final total of £237 12s. 1d. a small amount when set against the debts outstanding.

The descriptions in the Auction Book are not, perhaps, as full as the ceramic student would wish—there are several lots of "ornaments" and "vases", and one is a little at a loss to visualise exactly what these might be. Nevertheless, it is clear that ornamental items were very much in the minority. There are only four or five lots of figures and the single bust, and there are no items listed as "china cottages" or "poodle dogs", which while in no way conclusive, is additional evidence for the view that cottages and poodles were not made at the Rockingham Pottery. The quantity of earthenware was very considerable.

A photocopy of the Auction Sale Book may be consulted at the Rotherham Public Library.

Additional references:

a   (p. 108) The comport in Sheffield Museum is illustrated in *Collectors Guide*, Feb. 1965 p. 31, and in R. J. Charleston (Ed.) *English Porcelain* 1745-1850 (Benns 1965) Plate 55b.

b   (p. 111) An octagonal plate is illustrated in the Catalogue of the Schreiber Collection Vol. I (Porcelain) Plate 87.

c   (p. 111) See also G. A. Godden *Illustrated Encyclopaedia of British Pottery and Porcelain* (1966) especially pp. 271-7 dealing with Ridgways.

d   (p. 123) It has been established from the Minton factory pattern books that all these 'flat-backed' figures, except "The Boxers", should be ascribed to Minton *not* Rockingham.

INDEX

149

150

Notes—
  (i) The names of known Rockingham artists and workpeople are printed in *italics*.
  (ii) Detailed references to Rockingham wares are listed under EARTHENWARE and PORCELAIN.